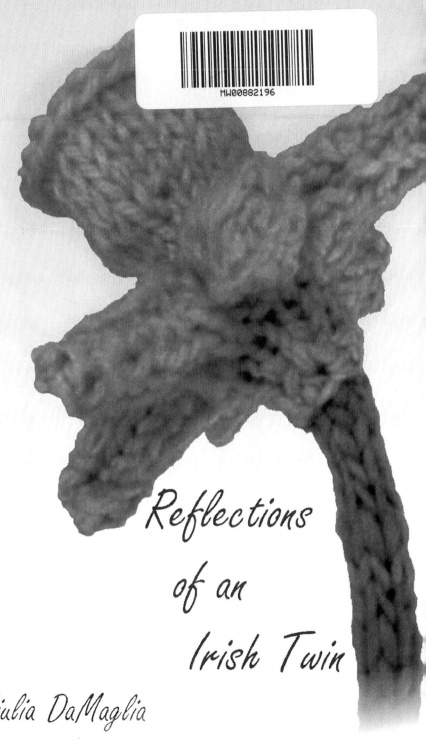

Reflections

of an

Irish Twin

Giulia DaMaglia

Dear Joyce,
How's the red bag coming along?
Thanks for listening!
Judy

ISBN: 1481271482

ISBN 13: 9781481271486

Library of Congress Control Number: 2013901062
CreateSpace Independent Publishing Platform
North Charleston, South Carolina

DEDICATION

*My work here is dedicated to my twin grandsons.
I have known, hugged and loved you since fifteen
minutes after you were born. You've given me more
happiness than you will ever understand. Both of
you excel in academics, sports and caring for others.
You are funny characters. I predict both of you will
achieve personal satisfaction and contribute much to
society. How did I get so lucky?*

*AND to my husband, the most intelligent, patient
and understanding guy in the whole world!*

All my love!
G.

REFLECTIONS OF AN IRISH TWIN

BY GIULIA DAMAGLIA

TABLE OF CONTENTS

INTRODUCTION

Lots of people have been told, "You should write a book." Everyone has at least one story to tell. It was time for me to take the plunge and put my own writing on paper for others to enjoy. It's my goal that the reader be reminded of his/her life's experiences and perhaps feel a comfortable sense of 'coming home.'

While this book is based on some true events that the author remembers, those events have been fictionalized and all persons appearing in this work are fictitious. Any resemblance to real people living or dead is entirely coincidental.

ACKNOWLEDGMENTS

One might think that writing is a lonely or solitary exercise. It isn't!

I sit down at my work table with six sharpened pencils, a pad of writing paper and the people and events I remember, imagine or invent begin to gather around me. My work space becomes crowded and busy with the characters, real or imagined, that I am writing about. I am surrounded by the people I've created!

Of course, there are real people who have been a part of this writing adventure to whom I am most grateful:

Doc. Judy offered a writing course at the community center near where I live. I enrolled because I needed a stimulus to get started. After two sessions, I was off and running and writing far more than what individual class time presentations allowed. I appreciate her presence in my life and writing efforts.

The members of my Knit-wit club, the members of my book club, my sister-friends and my husband who never turned a deaf-ear when I wanted to read something I had recently written to them.

My fine-artist neighbor, Martha; my graphics artist friend, Spencer; and the 'one and only' Clay for their unique and creative contributions to my work.

Editor Annette. She thrilled and inspired me with her words of praise and encouragement. How lucky for me that I found her!

Atty. Michael M. for advice and counsel.

Finally, Priscilla for her technical skills, patience and love.

Apologies to Angus!

CHAPTER 1

What is an Irish Twin?

It's as if Alfred Adler knew me personally, for it is uncanny how accurately he describes my personality. Adler (1870-1937) was a medical doctor, a psychologist and a contemporary of Freud and Jung who theorized that one's birth order has more to do with personality development than any other variable. Of course, there are other researchers who have disputed this claim. However, he seems to describe me, a firstborn, as having the following traits:

- needs to have everything under control
- has an aggressive nature and is driven
- needs to be perfect
- needs to be in charge
- needs to be on time and on schedule
- makes lists
- is scholarly and logical
- is reliable and conscientious.

Adler further analyzed what happens when a second child comes along while the firstborn is still an infant. Adler posits that the older children in this instance work all their lives to please others in an attempt to regain the attention and praise that was solely theirs before the second child came along and dethroned her/him.

The term "Irish twins" was originally a derogatory label attached to the children of Irish, Catholic, immigrant families in the 1800s born within one year of each other. The Irish were thought to be backwards, uncultured, uneducated, and unable to use birth control. They had children one right after another because they were irresponsible about planning ahead and controlling themselves.[1] Today the phrase does not carry a pejorative meaning. It simply refers to two siblings born to the same mother less than twelve months apart.

Mother Nature, I believe, meant for siblings to be spaced at least two years apart. By that time, siblings have enough separation from each other and need not fight for parental attention and their own individuality. Dr. John McDermott, former chairman of Psychiatry at the University of Hawaii Medical School, suggests that an ideal spacing is two and a half to three and a half years. He claims that shorter intervals often produce more intense sibling rivalry[2]. When an infant is breast-fed exclusively for two years (no supplemental feedings), a woman's ovaries are unlikely to produce an egg and therefore no fertilization can occur. Granted, breast feeding is not a 100% birth control method, but the hormones necessary to produce breast milk generally decrease the advent of ovulation. Certainly in caveman times, babies were nursed until they had enough teeth to chew rare meat and raw vegetables. There were no jars of Gerber baby food in the cave's kitchen cabinets.

My mother said she tried to breast feed but didn't succeed. I became a bottle-fed baby and she became fertile. I think I now know why she couldn't breast feed. For some reason, when I drink from a cup or glass, I keep my tongue above the lip. Since I have done

---

1   Irish Twins. July, 2012. In Wiketionary Online. Retrieved from: en.Wikipedia.org/wiki:Irish_Twins

2   McDermott, John. The Complete Book on Sibling Rivalry. Putnam. 1987. p. 5

this all my life I probably did this as a newborn. With my tongue up, I wouldn't have been able to suck or latch onto the breast. In the early 1940s new mothers started following the trend of the rich and famous whose babies were bottle-fed. Hospital nurseries had regimented schedules about when babies could come out to the mothers for feedings. Perhaps little Giulie came out when she wasn't hungry. Then back in the nursery I would scream bloody murder because now I was hungry. So I would be given a supplemental bottle feeding and I then had no interest in breast feeding the next time I came to my mother. Perhaps even then I needed to be "in charge," but the nursery staff wouldn't let me keep to my own schedule! Under these circumstances, it is unlikely that anyone from the obstetrical staff was available during the five-day lying-in postpartum period to diagnose that the placement of my tongue prevented my mother from nursing successfully. Thus, I'm inclined to believe that I caused myself to become an Irish twin. I wouldn't have done that had I known the consequences!

To be clear: I am not really Irish. I have one great-grandmother named Bridget who crossed the Irish Sea and married my great-grandfather William. William and all other ancestors on my maternal and paternal sides of the family came from Lancashire, England and almost all of them worked as laborers in the cotton mills.

What must be obvious by now is that I am not a twin, either.

Some blogs would have you think that having Irish twins is the way to go. They are written by mothers who don't know or feel the actual experience that children so close in age actually have.

The second sibling (a sister) came along when I was eleven months old. At that tender age, it is speculated by psychologists that a child such as I couldn't understand why things were different. My parents, particularly my mother must have been exhausted. She had two babies in diapers, two babies that had to be fed and when she put us together in a playpen for safekeeping and some peace, I would use my sister's arms and legs as a teething ring. Surely, I didn't earn any "brownie points" when my mother saw teeth marks on my sister. Neither at that tender infantile age nor throughout most of my adult life did I understand or internalize what was driving my behaviors. By instinct though I realized that in order to survive, I must please my parents (particularly my mother) and all others in authority.

As Christmas approached this past year, I told my knitting students, "Please don't give me gifts." A dear friend, Penny, said, "You can't do that. Your students are grateful for what you do for them and want to please you and express their gratitude." "Honestly, I don't know how to handle that," I replied. Her answer was, "Be gracious and just say 'thank you.'" The basic problem, we concluded, is that I have to be the one to please others. **I** need to be in charge of who's pleasing whom. Understanding the origin of this personality characteristic, I will now submit, and be gracious. **I** now appreciate that others may need to please me as much as **I** need to please them. I should not deny the need that others have when that same need has been so important to me. My eyes are open now, so bring on the presents!

In general, the traits I likely developed as a first-born and being an Irish twin did serve me well though most of my life and during my career(s). But upon retirement I discovered that the behaviors that worked for me in the past were no longer needed and were probably a deterrent to my being happy. Now I was no longer "in charge" of anybody. That fact was brought to my attention when I was diagnosed and treated for breast cancer. It was expected that I meet with a psychiatric nurse practitioner for a few sessions as part of a team treatment regimen. (See Chapter 10.) I assumed I'd get a pat on the back for handling the diagnosis of cancer so well. Instead, early into my first session I was spilling my guts about everything and everybody that bugged me. In our second session, the therapist gently offered her assessment of me: "Your mother brought you up to be a fighter. You need to give that fighting spirit and your need to be a perfectionist back to your mother. You don't need those attributes any more. Stop expecting others to be as reliable, punctual and as thorough as you are because most people will soon disappoint you. Other people are not like you."

According to Dr. Kevin Leman,[3] another developmental psychologist, "Whatever the first born in a family is like, the second born will likely go in the entirely opposite direction." To be sure, it couldn't have been easy or pleasant to be my younger sister by only eleven months. We started school the same year. That was a mistake. She was always being compared to me. Teachers would question her asking, "Why can't you be more like your sister, Giulia? Look at how well Giulia does; you could do well, too, if you tried harder." They would ask me why I wasn't helping my sister to do better. (Did teachers not have any psychology courses back then? Didn't they understand how insensitive those questions/statements were?) I complained to my mother about having to shoulder these remarks. She advised that I say, "I am not my sister's keeper." That sounded reasonable on the surface, but even she implied on occasion, "Your sister is not stupid, but she doesn't always use good judgment." What did she expect me to do?

My sister, Pam and I were assigned to different units at Girl Scout camp one summer. A counselor from my sister's unit came to get me because Pam wouldn't come out of her tent to eat her hot dog. That's when I should have said, "But I'm not my sister's keeper." But dutifully, I went to see what I could do. Pam said she wasn't coming out of the tent to eat because her friend, Barbara, didn't like hot dogs and she, Barbara, decided the two of them should not eat hot dogs. Loyal Pam planned to stay in the tent with Barbara. I told Pam that word would get to Mom about what she was doing because Mom's office was only down the hall from the Girl Scout office. Mom would not be happy that she was behaving that way. So, reluctantly, she joined the others for hot dogs. I don't know what Barbara did.

My sister and I walked to Sunday school and Junior Church each week with an envelope for the collection plate. Our envelopes

---

3   Leman, Kevin. The first Born Advantage. Revell. 2008 p. 28

each contained a dime. At the top of the street, my sister would tear open the envelope and pocket the dime. I, of course deposited my envelope in the plate as expected. Tuesday was bank day all during our school years. My mother gave each of us twenty five cents to turn in. The teachers would enter the twenty five cents on cards which would be deposited into a local bank. At the end of the school year the bank books would be given to us to keep over the summer should we wish to add additional funds. My statement would show faithful deposits of twenty five cents weekly while my sister's would be blank.

Having a sister so close in age was often times irritating. I never felt that I had any space of my own. It seemed like she was always behind me and breathing down my neck all through childhood. My mother's rule was that wherever we went, we had to leave together and come home together. Don, a boy in our high school homeroom, would ask one of us for a date to a school dance. Following my mother's instructions, when Don arrived to pick us up, we would both get in his car. My sister would sit next to him going and I would sit beside him coming home. He was a gentleman about all this. Many years later, at a high school reunion, I asked what he thought about that arrangement. He said, "Are you kidding? I thought it was fabulous. I had two dates by only asking one. It was like I had hit the jackpot."

On the other hand, having a sister so close in age did have some advantages. For example, we always had someone to go places with. We didn't have to import playmates and we shared inside jokes, nicknames and a common family history that never needed to be explained. Also, my sister would often acquiesce to helping me get what I wanted. "Please nominate me and vote for me to be patrol leader," I would ask. She would agree to do that because she had no desire to lead. She preferred to follow. I encouraged her to promote me and she usually did. For that, I remain grateful. I, on the other hand, never squealed about her transgressions. (Chapter 2 tells more of the relationship between me and my Irish twin.)

Finally, with this examination of birth order affecting personality characteristics, I must mention the third and last sibling who was born four and a half years after me. The literature describes later-borns as unconventional, adventurous and rebellious because they have a lesser attachment to their parents and suffer from domination by older siblings. For being the family "underdog," later-borns tend to identify with the downtrodden.[4]

Where she was born so many years after me, it was as if she was of a different generation—and even from another planet. I can relate to the rebellious characteristic, for we hardly ever had a family meal without her starting a brouhaha. My mother's rule was that we must eat two bites of each food item on our plate. All the dishes would be cleared, washed and put away and sister Carol would still be sitting at the table refusing to take those obligatory bites. Then my father would start, "You're too demanding of her."

"Why? What's required for the others should apply to her too." It would usually end with a "Go to bed" followed by lots of door slamming. (How that door ever stayed on its hinges is a mystery to me.) Perhaps one could connect her identification with the downtrodden with the fact that she pursued a career in counseling the mentally disabled. She loved her work.

In reviewing these theories on birth order and the strong determination of personal characteristics, my husband (an engineer) asked, "Does that mean there's no such thing as self determination? Are we cast in stone?" I'm not a psychologist, but I believe we are molded and shaped by our birth order and childhood experiences. It seems like it is not until adulthood that many of us discover the stuff in our personal makeup that we'd prefer to do without. Change is the answer to personal determination. Maybe that accounts for why there are so many self-help references on the shelves of bookstores, why psychiatrists and psychologists have so many clients and probably why Dr. Phil's TV program is so popular.

---

4   Oates, Stephen B. The Fires of Jubilee: Nat Turner's Fierce Rebellion. New York: Harper & Row. 1975. p. 126

CHAPTER 2

Growing Up

While not quoting Dr. Phil exactly, he would not likely quarrel with this statement: A family is the most complicated societal institution there is. Then there is the term *dysfunctional family* to consider. I grew up thinking my family was as normal as could be. Now, I'm not so sure. Although I wouldn't classify our family as dysfunctional, my parents hid from us the damaging marital problems that for them caused some unhappy and troublesome times.

Here then, is the cast of characters that appear in my family story as I was growing up.

- Father, Carl
- Mother, Harriet
- Oldest Daughter, Giulia, your humble author
- Second Born, Pam
- Third Born, Carol
- Carol's twin brother Carl, who premature like Carol, died shortly after birth
- A Half Brother, also named Carl
- Supporting Characters: Grandmothers and Aunts

CARL

Carl, the father, was quick-witted and funny when he had an audience. He drove a bus for over fifty years and many elderly and homeless passengers rode around and around on his route just to be entertained (and they only paid for one fare). He had nicknames for all his passengers, teased and joked with them, and on rainy days drove the bus down streets that were not on the route so folks wouldn't get wet walking home. He would "backfire" the bus in front of people's houses he knew—it's said that even some pets anticipated his time table and would be in the window waiting for him to come by. When Carl was in the hospital being treated for colon cancer, it was difficult for family members to visit because all of the visitors' passes had been given out to his bus passengers. Fortunately, I knew how to get to his room by some back stairs. There in his room were all these people who were total strangers to me. Some of them were not able to speak English, but there they were, nodding at my father praying, "Bless you Mr. Carl." At Christmas time, he came home with shopping bags full of gifts: many of them ugly ties or terribly smelling colognes. He treasured those gifts, I think, more than the ones we gave him.

In Carl's busman's bag that sat beside him when he drove the bus was a dated paystub from the 1930s. As a new driver, he would get up at four in the morning, go to the bus garage and wait to be put on a few runs for the day. Sometimes, he'd wait until noon to work. That yellowed paystub amounted to a total of $4.75. After the government took five cents for the federal old age fund, five cents for state unemployment insurance and the company took $1.50 for uniforms and $2.00 for union dues, Carl got $1.15. Carl told how a guy in front of him at the bank teller's window asked for his pay in small bills. So Carl approached the teller, presented his check of $1.15 and said, "I'll have mine in small bills, too."

Here are two stories that capture my father's quick wit: My sister, Pam, was a widow. When her children were all through college, married and had children of their own, she happened to be dating a guy named Jack. He turned out to be much older than he said AND he had strange habits. For example, he would dry out used paper towels on the shower curtain rod to reuse them. He reused tea bags umpteen times. After a few dates, Pam told him their relationship was over. He asked, "So does that mean I can't come to your mother's house on Sunday to celebrate my birthday?" She, of course said, "No way." At dinner that Sunday, my mother asked, "Now what am I supposed to do with the handkerchiefs I bought that have a 'J' on them?" My father quickly replied, "That's why I tell you to always buy handkerchiefs with an 'A.' That way you can give them to any asshole."

Very late one night when my parents were asleep, the phone rang. My mother got up to answer. When she returned to bed, my father asked who it was. "It was an obscene caller," she said.

"What did he want?"

"He wanted my body"

"Did you tell him to bring a U-Haul?"

Carl was indeed sharp and witty. He was also very fastidious and an impeccable dresser. Never did he have a hair out of place. Those who knew him would laughingly suggest that if he should look down and see a hole in his sock, he would have to park the bus, come home and change his socks. At the end of a workday, he would sit at the dining room table to count up the fares and report them on a special sheet provided by the bus company. First, he would sharpen his pencil to a fine point by rubbing it on one of the slats under the table (the slats where we would occasionally hide food we didn't want to eat). Then he would meticulously enter the numbers on the tally sheet. When he did crossword puzzles, each letter was entered right into the middle of each box – never on any lines. Likewise, his car, when he finally had one, was shiny, washed regularly and always had a full tank of gas. One weekend, when I was home from college, I borrowed the car to do some errands downtown. Unfortunately, I backed up into a hydrant and made a small dent in the back fender. The dent was not visible from the house and

I went back to school without telling him and without his noticing it. I did, however, tell my mother, who then told him after I left. She explained that I was scared about telling him and was having stomach aches about it. He sent me a letter along with some toilet paper saying, "It's OK and here's something for your diarrhea." Incidentally, his penmanship was perfect and lovely to look at even though he never finished high school. He said he never graduated from high school because he skipped class too much. "The only time I got 75 on my report card was for the number of times absent."

My father didn't correspond often. But one Thanksgiving after I was married, he sent me a note with instructions on how to cook a turkey. "Fill the cavity with popcorn kernels. Roast it in the over at 325 degrees. When the ass blows off, the turkey is done." That following Christmas, to reciprocate, I lined a box with tissue paper and filled it with popcorn. At my mother's house I took the rear end off the turkey she had cooked, placed it on top of the popcorn and wrapped the package up with beautiful paper and ribbon. The tag said, "To Carl from Santa." Carl opened it with enthusiasm and curiosity. Seeing what was there, he put it aside and said not a word. He preferred being the joker, not the recipient of a joke.

At home alone with my mother, he was not as full of charm and wit as he was out in public. Perhaps this is the case with many men/husbands. He wanted peace and quiet and a regular routine. He could sleep on a picket fence and be revived after a half-hour nap.

Carl was surrounded by women: a wife and three daughters. The third daughter was a twin, whose brother died shortly after birth. He would have been a Carl, Jr. His death certificate lists the cause of death as prematurity (seven months) and atelectesis (collapsed lung), which today would likely be called Hyaline Membrane Disease. Certainly having a son may have changed the dynamics of our family in ways I can't even imagine. But, being a tomboy, I did some things with him that he might otherwise have done with a son. For example, there were our fishing expeditions.

Together, we would ride our bikes to the bottom of a steep hill where we lived and head towards the banks of a river. He carried a shovel and I had our hand fishing lines and a bucket in my bike's basket. We wore bathing suits under our shorts and jerseys. At the river's edge, we dug for sea worms. (They were pinkish ugly things with pincers on their heads.) Cutting them in pieces to put on my fishing hook didn't bother me in the least, although I left the head end for my father to deal with. With about a dozen worms in my bucket, we hid the shovel under some bushes and continued along the river's edge until we came to the remains of an old railroad bridge. There we would sit on the railroad trestle, bait our hooks, drop the hand lines and wait for bites. We caught small sunfish and scup none ever big enough to bring home for eating. I wanted my father to be proud of the way I could bait my own hooks, back the hooks out of a fish's mouth whenever I caught one and throw it back into the water. I tried to be like a son to him. After fishing for a while, we'd dive off the trestle and swim. My father liked to lie on his back, bring his knees up to his chest, dunk his head back, fill his mouth with water and then spout it out at me as if he were a whale. At the end of the day, we'd retrieve the hidden shovel and start back home, stopping at Eva's Variety Store to buy some penny candy. Sunburned and tired, we'd have to push the bikes back up that steep hill to get home. I felt special and very close to my father on those occasions. They were lovely days. They were perfect days.

One time, however, he went fishing without me. He got the fishhook stuck in his right hand. Fishhooks have a barb on them so they cannot be pulled back out. Fishhook in his hand still attached to the fishing line, he peddled the bike to the hospital about three miles away. The emergency room physician numbed his hand, clipped the hook and pushed it the rest of the way out. He was given a tetanus shot and sent home via bicycle. A week later Carl received a note from the physician who treated him. "Here is the fish hook we removed from your hand. What did you want us to do with the dead fish that is stinking up the place?" (There was no fish.

He never even got to the river that day.) Obviously, my father had given the emergency room staff something to chuckle about. As usual, he left an audience laughing.

I never heard Carl ever say anything about not having a son to rear. In fact, he was quite proud of his girls. When graduating from my college nursing program, I had a formal picture taken in my cap and uniform for the yearbook. I ordered an 8x10 tinted copy for my parents. My father carried that picture with him on the bus to show all the passengers. He earned the right to be proud after all the trials and tribulations of being a father to three daughters.

His daughters were sometimes an irritation. As mentioned previously, Carl was fastidious about himself and his possessions. That included his safety razor. He knew exactly how many shaves he could get before needing to insert a new blade. However, when one of us needed to shave our underarms or our legs, his razor was handy, sharp and inviting. So we helped ourselves to his razor instead of our own when he wasn't around. The next time he shaved, he'd be all lathered up and come out of the bathroom quite angry and with a raised voice ask, "Who's been using my razor? It's not as sharp as it should be and now I've nicked myself. I've asked all of you a hundred times not to use my razor." "Yes, Dad, but I was out of blades." "Well I'm telling you—don't use my razor anymore."

On Sunday mornings, we three girls dressed for church. There were no pantyhose then—just stockings with seams. They were held up with garter belts, which were easy for us to hook in the front. The tricky part was to fasten the backs of the stockings to belt hooks while keeping the seams straight. Some Sundays we were like an assembly line: the three of us standing in a line with our skirts hoisted up so my father could come down the line and hitch up the backs of our stockings. I just assumed that's what all fathers did for their daughters, but I realize now that Carl was one of a kind and we three had straight seams! (Lest one should wonder, he never, ever touched us inappropriately.)

Carl was not a handyman. If you asked him to fix something, he would always reply, "I only have a hammer and a screw driver. What do you expect me to do with them, build a house?" Napping was probably Carl's favorite pastime. He would sneak off, nap on the couch, and avoid chores whenever possible. After Christmas one year, Harriet was waiting for him to help take down the artificial tree and pack away the ornaments. She found Carl asleep on the couch next to the Christmas tree. Irritated, Harriet picked up the whole tree, ornaments and all, and carried it across the living room right past napping Carl. Then she opened the door to the basement and heaved the whole thing down the cellar stairs. When Carl woke up and noticed the tree was gone, he asked where the tree was. Harriet told him to check the cellar stairs. I don't know what Carl's reaction was, but we teased Harriet about that tree for many, many years.

Carl usually had a nice vegetable garden every year with corn, strawberries, string beans, tomatoes and potatoes. We picked and ate the corn before it was ready, so I don't know if it was any good or not. We shared a property line with a little Frenchman, named Mr. Charte. Mr. Charte gave my father two good-sized titaugh (white fish). My father had no idea how to clean or fillet them. He waited until dusk to go out to the garden to dig a hole and bury the fish. Mr. Charte came along and asked, "Mr. Carl, you want to use my shovel? It's bigger." Carl lied. He told Mr. Charte he was thinking about putting in a few more tomato plants and didn't need a bigger shovel for that. I'm not positive what my father did with the fish. He probably went around to the other side of the house where Mr. Charte couldn't see what he was doing.

Carl was pretty good at painting each house that we lived in. He'd be up the ladder in his shorts and a hat in the heat of a summer day getting a bad sunburn. His skin would peel off in strips and then he'd be a reddish tan for the rest of the summer. I must mention that he usually spilled at least one bucket of paint per project. The drive way was regularly adorned with the results of his artwork.

Here are some other skills Carl had:

- tightening up the little screws, to keep the bows on a pair of eyeglasses from falling off.
- polishing shoes—he especially liked whitening my nurses' shoes
- cooking steak on Thursdays (his day off)
- dancing
- playing imaginary drums on the kitchen table
- doing crossword puzzles and winning at Scrabble
- sticking out his upper dentures to amuse the grandchildren. They didn't realize his teeth were false and they tried for hours pushing against their front teeth with their tongues to imitate Carl.

Just when my parents might have begun to see the peace and quiet of their senior years, they became parents all over again. Pam was married to a career military serviceman. After three children, he was assigned to a tour of duty in Viet Nam. Pam decided that she and her children should move back into the homestead with my parents while her husband was overseas. He was not expected to be home for Christmas that year, so we mailed his gifts to him. At the last minute, he was informed he was on an approved list for R & R and did arrive to meet his family at my parents' home in time for the holidays. He was due to return to Viet Nam on New Year's Day. The day after Christmas, Pam and her husband went off to shop the post-holiday sales. Upon their return, he said he was tired and went to take a nap in the upstairs bedroom. At the bottom of the stairs, Pam heard a gurgling sound and rushed back up to find her husband all purplish and blue. As EMTs carried him out of the house on a stretcher, my father said to them, "This poor bugger is supposed to go back to Viet Nam on New Year's Day." One of the EMTs replied, "This poor bugger is going nowhere." My mother called me to ask that I get to the hospital immediately to see what comfort I could offer my sister. The emergency staff was still putting the paddles on him when I arrived, but it was too late: he had already died. Hearing this, Carl said, "Looks like I have to be a father all over again."

Harriet, my mother, asked that I stay the night and sleep with my sister. When I asked Pam what I could do for her, she requested two things. "Please tell my three kids what has happened. I don't know how nor do I want to. Also, go to the store and get me some cigarettes." I created an explanation about their dad based on each of their ages and stages of development. For example, I explained to the youngest, "You know how your dad likes to play golf? Well, now he has gone to a place in heaven where he'll be able to play golf every day if he wants to." I don't remember what I told the others, but Pam later thanked me saying that I must have explained things appropriately because the children were handling the situation well.

Their coping nicely with their father's death was also due, I believe, to the fact that they had been living with my parents while their father was in Viet Nam and were therefore not uprooted in any way. In fact, Pam and her children lived with my parents while her husband was stationed in Korea and then in Japan. Our family homestead was their homestead as well.

Thoughts of sickness/illness/deformities made Carl very nervous. When the bus company brought on busses with hydraulic lifts so wheel chair folks could get on and off the bus, he was panicky. He was afraid of what might be wrong with the person in the wheel chair. One day a rider had an epileptic seizure. Carl drove the bus to the nearest emergency room as if he were operating a rescue truck—blasting the horn all the way and tearing through the streets. The worst episode occurred, I believe, when Pam and Carol were fighting over the phone. They were having a tug-of-war with it when suddenly Carol let it go and it slammed into Pam's two front teeth chipping off a chunk from each tooth. Harriet was out at a meeting that evening and when Carl saw Pam's broken teeth, he nearly went berserk. Seeing him so out of control affected me the worst. I ran to a corner living room chair and curled up in it like a ball. Carl said, "What the hell's the matter with you?" I could only say, "I'm very scared." All of this was too much for Carl. He called Harriet to come home immediately.

Within their financial resources, my parents and a recommended dentist did everything they could do so save those teeth. First, they were capped, but the teeth died and were removed. Two false teeth were made and hooked onto the two teeth next to the missing ones. Gradually those two teeth developed problems and eventually all her upper teeth were extracted and she ended up with military-issue, one-size-fits-all dentures. Pam stopped smiling after that accident. She was always embarrassed by her teeth.

In my third year of my collegiate nursing program, I was scheduled to scrub on a chest case during my surgical rotation. The patient had lung cancer after smoking for many years. When I told my father about how black, bloody and mean looking those lungs were, he never smoked again. But, when he was closing in on age seventy, he must have had some symptoms of colon cancer such a bloody or tar colored stools, which he probably ignored. When visiting my aunt in New York, he fell in the bathroom and banged his head on the window sill. He couldn't remember what happened. The next time I saw him I coaxed him to see our doctor. "Suppose something like that happens while you're driving the bus? You could be responsible for injuring or killing other people." That was the thought that drove him to the doctor soon after. Blood work revealed he was bleeding somewhere and it turned out to be in his colon from cancer. I was there when the doctor presented this news along with the fact that he would be scheduled for surgery to have that section of his colon removed. He asked, "Will I be able to play the piano afterwards?" "Of course," replied the doctor. "That's good because I never could before." My mother, Harriet, got annoyed. "Carl, this is no time for joking." Next Carl asked, "Will I have to sit on a bag while I drive the bus?" Again, Harriet thought he was joking – but he wasn't. My father only had a vague idea of what a colostomy bag was. He thought it was something attached to one's anus that meant you would have to sit on it. The doctor knew what he was asking and told Carl it was unlikely he would be getting a colostomy. He claimed the surgeon believed all the cancer could be removed without his having to create a colostomy. That message was music to our ears.

Carl had his surgery, recovered nicely and happily went back to driving the bus and enjoying his passengers. They were thrilled to have him and his smiling face back again. Sadly, however, cancer cells were still in his body multiplying and eventually made themselves known by raising havoc in Carl's colon and other tissues. Another operation was performed and this time a colostomy was necessary. Carl asked the surgeon, "Did you get it all this time?" "No, I'm afraid the cancer has spread." was the reply. One of my nursing colleagues was there when Carl was given the news. She said my father came close to passing out and started trembling. Then he regained his composure and quietly began his days and months of coping with his last stage of life. He was offered radiation and chemotherapy. He accepted the former but not the chemo. "I don't want chemo because I know what it has done to others. It makes you sick for two or three weeks, you get one week of being just ok and then it's time for your next dose and you get sick all over again. I don't think it's worth it, do you, Giulia?" I could only reply that it was his life and his body. "You know what's best for you. You know what you can cope with and what you can't."

So my mother and Carl learned how to deal with the colostomy. Carl had all his radiation treatments and did go back to driving the bus for a short period of time before he officially retired. At home, he became weaker and thinner. It was so sad to see my dear and wonderful dad lying in his bed with cancer, knowing medical services were unable to save him.

My father lost his battle with colon cancer. While still at home, the visiting nurse came by three times a week to change the dressing, check his colostomy site, give him a bed bath and provide comfort measures. In between times, my mother did everything she could to keep him comfortable and at home. Sadly, they didn't have the wonderful services of Hospice available. When he said to me one day,

"I guess I'm buggered," I didn't know what to say. The worst thing he explained was knowing that he smelled like an 'old goat.' I did come up with an answer to one question he asked me: "Giulia, I'm ready to die. What's taking so long?" "You're a rugged guy and always have been. It's just not your turn yet." The day came when his condition had deteriorated to the point where the drainage from his colostomy and wound was not manageable. My mother and I took him to the oncologist. He took one look at the situation and wanted him admitted to a hospital. Unfortunately, there were no beds in the hospital he had been in several times before, so he was admitted to another hospital that for him was foreign. It was March, National Cancer Awareness Month where daffodils are sold to raise monies for cancer research. On the first evening of his hospital stay, someone placed a vase of unopened daffodils on his bedside table. Where he was scared, alone and unhappy with where he was, my father didn't sleep all night. Instead, he watched the daffodils open ever so slowly – bit by bit all during the night. His story about those daffodils made me feel so sad and I could not enjoy the beauty of a daffodil ever thereafter. Last spring one of my knitters, in appreciation of some finish work I did for her, gave me a small pot of miniature daffodils. She didn't know my distaste for those flowers, nor did I tell her. When the blooms started to wilt, I separated the roots and stuck them unceremoniously in the ground in my front courtyard. Early this spring those plants stuck their heads out of the ground and produced an array of pretty, dainty and cheerful flowers. "For God's sake, what are you doing?" I asked. "Don't you know I don't like you?" As I considered their persistence, I told myself, "Get over it! Those daffodils are telling you to remember happy times not the sad ones."

HARRIET

Harriet, my mother, was beautiful. Looking through her yearbook one day, I asked if anyone ever told her how beautiful she was. She said, "No – never." The father of one of the girl scouts in my troop remarked once that my mother was plain and very, pretty. She was pleased when she heard that. Perhaps the adjective 'plain' referred to the fact that she never wore makeup. She had her hair permed regularly – that's all. She was all about the needs of others and her own needs came last. Harriet was the brains, taskmaster, disciplinarian and goal setter of the family. She also had a sense of humor that was overshadowed my father's. We only saw that more clearly after he passed away. She taught me how to sew and she quietly cheered all my achievements in academics, sports and with needlework and crafts. It was later in life that I came to understand why her cheering for me had to be done quietly. It had to have been a schizophrenic experience for her to be happy that I won or succeeded at something and sad that Pam had failed. For example, in our junior year of high school, I tried out for the varsity basketball team and Pam wanted to be a majorette. I made it as a guard on the team, but Pam wasn't chosen for the majorette or cheerleading squad – not even as an alternate. She was bitter, complaining and crying. This was the typical dilemma my mother had to deal with for having Irish twins. She was happy for me but where my news was good, she had to focus more of her attention on the hurt my sister was feeling. Harriet was the middle of five children so she had a special empathy for Pam who was a middle child also. I didn't appreciate my mother's situation then and at times felt a bit shortshrifted. I craved my mother's approval and attention but it was often constrained.

Harriet grew up in difficult times – with times and challenges that I have never had to experience myself. Only eleven when the depression occurred, she and the whole family would probably have been less affected if the father, Thomas, hadn't been drunk as often as he was. Thomas was a master of mill machinery functioning. My father, who also worked for a short time in the mills said that Thomas would be 'half in the bag' but could still see that an eye hook on the ceiling was off by a half inch. My grandmother, Harriet's mother, tried many strategies to salvage and get his salary brought home. He earned a respectable income and could easily have kept the family afloat and survive more comfortably during the depression. Harriet's older brother had to cram his feet into his mother's shoes even in cold weather to stand in the bread lines for handouts. Grandma sometimes waited outside the mill where Thomas worked to get hold of his pay before he lost it in a nearby barroom. She even resorted to making hooch in her kitchen to get him to come home to drink. Nothing worked and she eventually filed for divorce when Harriet was twenty-three and I had just been born. With divorce pending, Thomas slit his wrists and died in a downtown boarding room. Because of Thomas' drinking problems, no alcohol ever crossed the threshold of our home. Harriet said that when her father was sober he was a very dear man. But after drinking, he was boisterous and unbearable. The children stayed out of sight so they wouldn't have to listen to him or stimulate his outbursts. If Harriet were riding home on the bus and saw her father about to get on, she would squat down behind one of the seats so he wouldn't see her and cause her embarrassment.

Thomas and his four siblings all came from the industrial town of Lancashire, England. Their mother hailed from Ireland, crossed the Irish Sea and married their father. She was Catholic and he Protestant. So their marriage agreement was that the boy children would be raised Protestant and the girls Catholic. Interestingly, Thomas' mother ended up buried in the Catholic cemetery of her adopted city and the father was interred in the Protestant one. One of Thomas' younger sisters was engaged to marry before coming to the United States. Her fiancé would follow when she had settled in. But when the time came, he wasn't allowed to enter this country because he had 'bowed legs.'

Harriet was hard working. I can't ever remember seeing her at rest or relaxing. My earliest memories go back to when we lived on the second floor of a three decker tenement. My mother had a wringer-type clothes washing machine in the bathroom. I can still hear her saying over and over again, "Keep your fingers away from the wringer."

When the wash was ready to dry, she would lean out the bathroom window to attach the clothes to a pulley line with clothespins.

In freezing weather clothes would be frozen on the line before she got to the next piece. Of course, her fingers were frozen, also. Occasionally the line would break and the clothes would fall to the ground getting all dirty. She'd have to start the washing all over again. She would cry out of frustration and that bothered me a lot because I didn't really understand what would make my mother cry. Another early memory was watching her at the sewing machine. I was fascinated by the needle going up and down making seams on a garment. One time I got too involved and turned the wheel of the machine so that the needle went down into her finger. When I saw the blood and heard her startled 'ouch.' I felt like hell.

When Pam and I started school and there were babysitting arrangements for the youngest sister, Harriet applied for a job as a legal secretary. For her interview she wore a black dress and I thought she looked fabulous. She got that job and worked for that lawyer, Mr. Beal for over forty years. She really liked him because his nature and disposition was always the same – never up and never down. He had an amazing vocabulary and Harriet, who was fond of language and poetry, would look forward to learning new words when she took dictation from him. Once the 'word of the day' was *inchoate*. Taking dictation, she would have to write it as it sounded and then look it up to spell it and understand it correctly. (*Inchoate* – imperfectly formed or developed, such as, an *inchoate* idea)

College was not an option for Harriet. She studied the commercial curriculum in high school. Her favorite subject was English – especially poetry. She could recite the "Wreck of the Hesperus" from beginning to end. Here's her favorite poem:

Mother Doesn't Want a Dog
By Judith Viorst

Mother doesn't want a dog.
Mother says they smell,
And never sit when you say sit,
Or even when you yell.

And when you come home late at night
And there is ice and snow,
You have to go back out because
The dumb dog has to go.

Mother doesn't want a dog.
Mother says they shed,
And always let strangers in
And bark at friends instead,
And do disgraceful things on rugs,
And track mud on the floor,
And flop upon your bed at night.
And snore their doggy snore.

Mother doesn't want a dog.
She's making a mistake,
Because, more than a dog, I think
She will not want this snake.

Her love of language was a big help to me when I was studying. She would be ironing in the kitchen quizzing me on French and Latin vocabulary while I ate my breakfast. There were many rhymes, connections and prompts she would suggest to help me memorize things. She critiqued my writing and could even help with algebra and geometry. Solving for "x" or "y" was unfamiliar, but her keen understanding of mathematical computations, ratios and common sense led her to simple algebraic solutions. I missed her coaching at college, but I had a great roommate who was an excellent study partner.

Harriet could always see another use for something other than what its original purpose was. The plastic ring caps that cover the opening of milk and juice containers I use to crochet around to make buttons or flower pins. I think of my mother every time I do that because it's something she might have done. She always had a cool idea to solve a problem. "What if you put an egg carton on the bottom of that basket so the fruit will stand up higher?" "Why not put an appliqué over that spot to cover up the stain or a spot of bleach?" "Could you braid some of the fabric left over from sewing the drapes to make a throw pillow?" She was clever. She made a lot of our clothes and most of our prom and special occasion dresses.

My mother was ambitious for us. She said out of three girls she wanted at least one English teacher. That didn't happen. I became a professor of nursing and my youngest sister went to college to major in special education. Pam didn't go to college. She got pregnant instead.

My father never hit us. Most of the time he didn't know we did anything wrong. But frustrated with us sometimes, Harriet spanked. One night we were horsing around long after we should have been asleep and she'd had enough. She said, "Maybe this will give you the message" and proceeded to spank us. Stupid me said, "You gave her one less than you gave me." "Alright, then, I'll give you two more!" Child psychologists say that spankings are harmful. I'm none the worse for being spanked and I do think kids have a knack for pushing parents to the breaking point.

Harriet made sure we got to see or participate in everything that was going on. She would say, "We'll go 'cause that way we get to see what everyone else sees. One day she took the three of us to a parade. Baby sister Carol was in the carriage while Pam and I held onto each side of it. At one point my mother noticed that I was chewing gum. "Where did you get that gum?" "I picked it off the sidewalk when the clown was going by." "Spit that out. That was in someone else's dirty mouth and now you might get sick." She pushed that carriage with one of us riding and other two holding on all over our section of the city: grocery shopping, to the park, etc. I'm sure she went through several sets of wheels.

Harriet had a nice singing voice and would have loved to have taken piano lessons. Her mother could only afford for one child to study piano. That privilege went to her younger sister who was then supposed to give my mother a duplicate lesson. She did learn to play a little bit. We loved her playing and singing: *Shine Little GlowWorm, Glimmer, Glimmer*.

In general, my mother enjoyed pretty good health most of her life until she developed polymyocitis[5] in her early seventies. The disease weakened the large muscles of her body, making it difficult to get out of a chair or to walk long distances. When it was suggested that she would qualify for a handicapped parking sticker for her car she said, "No way. I will get where I need to go without any help from a parking sticker." She was put on large doses of cortisone to slow the muscle destruction. The two of us eventually went to a specialist at a major city hospital who determined she had 'turned the corner' and could start being weaned off the cortisone. But cortisone, while a miracle drug, has many negative side effects. After her ordeal with polymyocitis, she became aware that some of the words she spoke were not what she intended. We didn't notice when she said something like 'suitcase' instead of 'windowsill.' That problem was caused by clogged carotid arteries, which were corrected by surgery. After that she had a bout of gout which should have been picked up on her pre-surgical blood work. I believe her long term treatment with cortisone weakened her immune system, for subsequently she developed shingles. The suffering she experienced was intolerable and she tried to bear up without complaint. But all that cortisone and all that pain certainly weakened her heart. One evening Pam was at the house. They were planning to have dinner together. Harriet said, "I'm sorry, but I don't feel like eating right now. I'm going to rest on the couch in the living room." A short time later, when she went to get up to go to the bathroom, she collapsed on the floor. The last thing she said was, "Call 911." Pam tried to do CPR and even if she knew how, it wouldn't have worked. Pam called me and I met her and my mother (who was deceased before she got to the hospital) in the emergency room. Pam had already rejected an autopsy being

---

5 An inflammatory muscle disease causing weekness of skeletal muscles. The symptoms develop gradually.

done. I regret she did that. I'd have liked to know for sure that it was a massive heart attack (myocardial infarction).

We arranged for Harriet to be transferred to the funeral home that our family always used and agreed to meet the funeral director at the family home to get further instructions. Pam said, "I'm not calling Carol. You can do it. She gave Mom and Dad too much grief. She only came to visit when her husband said she could." (Sometimes months and months went by without my parents ever hearing from her.) I said I'd call Carol as soon as we had set up an appointment at the funeral home. However, a neighbor called Carol before I could, to report that an ambulance had taken Harriet away. When Carol arrived at the house she saw the funeral director's car in the driveway. She came screaming into the house saying, "Were you not going to tell me my mother died?" I tried to tell her that I would have called as soon as we had an appointment set up to plan funeral arrangements.

To this day, I find it queer that she could get to the house so quickly and want to get involved when Harriet had died when she rarely came by when her mother was alive. She did the same thing when my father was terminally ill. There she was pushing mashed potatoes into his mouth when he just wanted to die quietly. She hung pictures of Easter bunnies all over his room and called the doctor begging that Carl be given another transfusion. My mother and I were at the hospital when the doctor came in. "Are you the one who called asking for another transfusion to be given? I'm confused. I thought you and your father didn't want any further treatments to prolong life." "No it wasn't me," I replied. "Please ignore that call. It's not what Carl would want." Was I bitter? You bet I was. Why didn't she spend time with her father when it would have mattered?

Plans were made for Harriet's funeral service. She was to be cremated after the service and visiting hours at the funeral home. Carol wanted her children to be pall bearers. But there was nowhere to carry the body other than out the front door and around to the back door to be transported for cremation. Who carried or didn't carry the coffin was the least of my concerns – I was grieving. Today, Carol remains angry that her children didn't get to carry the coffin. Again, I wonder, "Why was it so important for them to carry their dead grandmother when they rarely came to see her when she was alive?" My mother once said that perhaps when those children got their driving licenses, they would then think to come by and visit her. If that did happen, it wasn't very often. At Christmas, my parents would go to the town where they lived (about thirty miles away) to mail their presents. Carol's husband dictated when she could have contact with her parents. There will be more about Carol later in the chapter.

Prior to visiting hours at the funeral home, a friend of Harriet's asked Pam if she could sing at the service. Pam said it would be ok. So we along with all the guests were sitting while the pastor gave his blessings. Then out from behind some tall artificial plants stepped this woman wearing sneakers, who started singing on and on in a wobbly, falsetto voice. I couldn't believe how awful it was! I kept my head down so I wouldn't laugh, but when I looked up momentarily and caught my friend Ella's laughing eyes, I nearly lost it. Something between grief and giggling actually caused me to snort.

There was a family reception back at the house afterwards. Everyone brought food including my Italian mother-in-law who sent lots of homemade pizza. Carol sent cupcakes via a nephew saying to him, "Have a good life." That was the last anyone saw or heard of her until I, as executrix, called a meeting to divide up my mother's personal belongings.

I missed my mother dreadfully. When someone you care for dies suddenly, there's no time to say how much you loved them or to thank them for all they did. You have to hope your actions and behaviors during your life successfully sent that message. My loss was profound. I couldn't knit for a whole year. Where knitting gives me peace, not being able to knit left me like a 'fish out of water.' I knit, sew, quilt and crochet like crazy now, with gratitude to my mother for giving me so much. She was a beautiful woman inside and out.

I executed my duties as executrix with diligence. At the end of her life my mother had been piling her papers in a laundry basket. I went through everything with a fine tooth comb to see what, if anything, I needed to do to clear up her affairs. Of course, a lawyer was hired to probate the will. (He tried to up his rates after we had agreed on a price!) I chased down insurance reimbursements, overpayment of a charge card and other credits she was entitled to. When checks came in I cried, "Mom, this is your money, what should I do with it?" Finally, Pam and I decided to use the money to buy a larger and prettier grave stone. It had ivy engraved into the corners to symbolize eternity. Before she died, my mother and I had a discussion about her will. She said that because Pam had no husband and because she used the insurance money from her husband's death to put a pool in the backyard, that she should leave the home to her. All I said at the time was, "It's your decision and your property. I don't think I should have a say in the matter." On a later occasion she said, "Pam isn't stupid, but she doesn't always use good judgment. Keep an eye out for her." She had shingles then and probably felt the end was near. I tried my best to help Pam, but it wasn't easy.

PAM

Pam didn't go to college. Instead she enrolled in a vocational-type program that prepares its students for employment in the airline industry as ticket agents, stewardesses, etc. At that time she was dating a guy in the air force who was between tours of duty in Japan and Korea. She became pregnant. I wish I hadn't been around that day when she came home with her significant other to tell my mother that she was getting married. My mother said, "No, you can't do that, you're too young." Pam replied, "But I have to – I'm pregnant." My mother went crazy. She hit the living room door so hard that the top half came off its hinges. They went somewhere to get married, her husband went off to Korea, and Pam dropped out of school and moved in with my parents.

Her husband was **not** a nice guy – good-looking yes – but a short-tempered and critical man. He drank a lot. After an afternoon of drinking, he arrived at my parents' home to pick up Pam for a date. I was lying on the living room couch studying. He suddenly lay down on top of me and said, "It's you I really love." "Get off of me," I demanded. I should have told Pam about that episode, but I didn't. I felt it would be too embarrassing for her. Chances are she was already pregnant at that time anyway. Pam's husband was always putting her down, telling her how cheap and lousy she looked and how stupid she was. After his death she admitted, "To be honest, I'm better off without him. He made my life miserable." She truly earned the benefits she received from the military for being an air force widow: medical/surgical insurance for her and her children, full four-year college tuition and expenses for each child and ten thousand dollars a year tax-free allowance.

Prior to the liaison with her first husband, Pam dated a guy named Wesley. He was on the wild side, smoking, speeding around in his souped-up car and encouraging Pam to skip school so they could go to the beach together. One night Pam said she was going to her friend's house to study. Carl and Harriet followed her and caught her taking off in Wesley's car filled with other teen agers. Pam was forbidden from ever seeing Wesley again and they kept close tabs on her to be sure she obeyed. Wesley comes back into the picture later on.

My mother's statement about Pam not using good judgment was right on the money.

For one thing, Pam would make decisions and act on them without considering the consequences or asking for advice. While covered by military insurance, she had a Pap smear that was positive for cancer cells. She proceeded to arrange for a hysterectomy with her own gynecologist at a private hospital. She got the bill and was shocked it wasn't covered by insurance because the surgery didn't take place in a military hospital. The bill was huge – more than she could ever afford to pay. "Please come to the military base with me to help fight this problem. You do all the talking." So I went and explained that when the word cancer comes up a woman has to go and be treated where she is most comfortable. I said more than that, but those words were the main message. The military officer left the room saying he'd be right back. When he returned, I started in again. "And another thing…" He stopped me there, "You needn't say anymore. We've decided to honor and pay the claim."

Once Pam applied for a receptionist job in a doctor's office while still in high school. The job required a typing speed of X number of words per minute. She didn't have typing expertise and was 'bent out of shape' when she didn't get the job.

I still wonder why, knowing she was pregnant, she would enter a city beauty pageant. Her talent was twirling a baton. She used to put an artificial freckle above her lip with an eye liner pencil. One of the judges asked if it was natural and Pam was 'ticked' that he should ask such a 'stupid' question. It baffles me how she could put more importance on the value of a fake freckle than on the possibility of being chosen "Miss City" and then having to reveal she wasn't eligible because she was pregnant.

Pam came to my rescue on two important occasions. I was set to start studies for my Master's Degree when my baby sitting plans fell apart. Pam agreed to take care of my little Ben. Her youngest was a little older, so they were often in the playpen together. My mother would meet me at a little white church before she went to work, to pick up Ben and take him to her house for Pam to take care of. At the end of the day, after school, I would then go to pick him up. I don't think she let Ben have a dirty diaper for more than ten minutes before she got him all cleaned up. She took really good care of him.

Another time when I separated from my first husband, she said I could stay at her house on the nights I needed to or when her children were not at home. Some nights I stayed there and other nights with a friend. My father was terminally ill in the hospital at that time, so some nights I slept in a recliner chair in his room. I was grateful for my sister's hospitality during that difficult time.

After Harriet died, Pam's behaviors became more and more strange and difficult to understand. Before the will was probated, Pam said, "This is my house. You can't come in without my permission." I explained that the house was not yet hers officially and I might enjoy coming back into the house that had been my home for so many years. She removed the key from where it had always been hidden. Pam inherited eighty-five percent of my mother's estate: the house and all my mother and father's IRAs. My youngest sister and I discovered that my mother had built up a savings account in the amount of one thousand dollars for each of the two of us. I couldn't believe it. How did she manage to do that? I reminded Pam that she needed to be prepared to pay taxes on the IRAs she inherited because it was money that went into savings without ever having been taxed. She was furious. "I wish I had just gotten one thousand like you did instead of IRA money." "Are you kidding," I thought to myself.

We three sisters met at the homestead one last time to divide up Harriet's personal belongings. Previously I mailed both sisters a pattern of choosing I developed that gave each of us equal opportunity to select what we'd like to have. I asked that all items chosen be moved out by a specific date so the house would be ready for Pam to move into. I called Pam to ask if she understood and thought the "choosing system" I developed was fair. She said, "I don't know, I threw it away." I thought that was very fresh, but I let it go. The divvying went without incident. Carol only wanted games, puzzles and stuff like that to use in her classroom. Pam and I selected pieces of furniture we wanted and I arranged for the Salvation Army to pick up everything that was left. The family home included an extra, buildable lot. First there was the house, next to it the driveway, and then the empty lot. We played badminton, horseshoes, had races, parties, etc. there. When Pam's oldest son married, they moved into a tiny attic apartment. They were cramped for space when their first child came along, so my mother sold this grandson the empty lot for one dollar. I think it was planned that as she aged, my mother would have someone nearby to check in on her. However, the grandson's wife was a high-strung, always yelling kind of woman who would sometimes walk right by my mother without even saying hello. She had a perpetual 'hair across her ass,' and all this bothered Harriet.

My mother had loaned Pam's daughter ten thousand dollars when she and her husband were about to purchase their first home. My mother told me there was an IOU regarding that loan in her papers. When I came across it, Pam grabbed it out of my hand, tore it up and said, "That was paid off."

Pam smoked. Being able to shop in the military BX made it easier to smoke because the price of cigarettes was so much cheaper. Pam said she'd like to quit but couldn't afford the medication. Interestingly the prescription used at that time was Wellbutrin, an antidepressant. For people with clinical depression, it was a drug covered by insurance. But for use to reduce the urge to smoke, it was called Zyban and not covered. We talked this over and I said, "I really care about your well-being and want to help you quit smoking. I'll pay for the medication." It was expensive and took two prescription refills – but it worked. She never smoked thereafter. I did this for her out of love and caring.

Pam moved into the homestead and began to consider plans to gut and reconfigure the whole house. I called her regularly to stay in touch and occasionally we got together for shopping or to go out for Chinese food. Then one time I called to learn that the number was temporarily disconnected. A few days later I went by the house to see what was going on. Pam happened to be there and happily showed me that the house was gutted. We both stood on the threshold of what had been the back door. When I looked in, I saw the dirt floor of the basement and the rafters of the ceiling three floors up – nothing in between. She talked excitedly about her house plans and gave me the number of where she was staying. We went back to getting together regularly. What she did with that old house was magnificent – the best of everything – spectacular in every way. Her inheritance of the house and the IRAs paid for her to have a palace-like home to live in. I was happy for her and enjoyed stopping by to visit some days on my way home from work. Things between us seemed to be fairly normal in spite of her occasional barbs such as, "You didn't do anything regarding Mom's estate that I couldn't have done." I let those kinds of comments go unanswered.

It turned out that Pam ran up a huge credit card debt buying all the appliances she wanted installed in her remodeled house. When she told me what she owed and what the interest charges were, I realized she would be paying on that debt forever and probably would cost her more than double the actual cost of the purchases. I gave her a twenty thousand dollar, interest free loan. She was to repay me in monthly installments. I forgave her December payment because she needed money for Christmas shopping and forgave the last two payments as a gift.

Sometimes we got together to walk. But she started getting pains in her feet and calves of her legs after shorter and shorter distances. She actually diagnosed her own condition via the internet as peripheral artery disease and a visit to a vascular surgeon confirmed that fact. The surgeon scheduled Pam for surgery. She got angry with her son who lived next door because he didn't "have the courtesy to call and see how I made out at the doctor's." So she decided she wasn't going to tell him about her upcoming surgery. I took it upon myself to contact her daughter and somehow got her to straighten out the rift between mother and son without bringing my name into the picture. Pam asked that I stay with her pre and post op. The morning of surgery, the physician came by to review the procedure and explain what to expect. Pam said to the surgeon, "Please tell all that to my sister, Giulia. She'll then tell me what I need to know." I stayed with Pam until she was on a stretcher being moved to the operating room. At that point she asked that I be there as soon as she came to the recovery room to put in her dentures. I took care of that request. She received her first get well cards while still in the recovery room. They were from my two children. I stayed with her each day she was in the hospital until one of her children arrived later in the day. She was receiving analgesia via a continuous caudal infusion. Unfortunately, that method was discontinued after twenty-four hours, but the surgeon neglected to order a substitute pain management therapy. When I showed up the next day, Pam was in agony. I hit the roof. I put in a call to the doctor for an immediate order for pain medication, instituted relaxation techniques (like Lamaze), and administered a reverse enema to remove any abdominal gas. No doubt I drove the staff crazy with my effort to get Pam comfortable. She was better when I left that day. My husband and I visited the next morning. I couldn't believe my eyes. Pam looked fabulous. There she was wearing makeup, looking relaxed and rested. When I entered her room she said, "Thanks a million. I could have died in this place and no one would have cared. I need to hug you. I love you!" My husband got into the act. "I didn't do anything, but could I have a hug too?" After discharge, I stayed with her each day from early morning until her son came home from work. When she was up to it, I took her on her first outing – to get a vanilla frosty.

During this time, it happened that her high school boyfriend, Wesley's wife died. She had been fighting cancer for many years. To Wesley's credit, his wife passed away in her own home with her husband and two sons by her side. When Pam was back on her feet, after having that major operation, she contacted Wesley to explain she wasn't able to come to his wife's funeral because of having had surgery. Wesley called and their relationship was rekindled. Between the time her husband died and she was reunited with Wesley, she had had relationships with many men. Some of them were married, others were losers and a few others were put off because they felt she was looking for a 'meal ticket.'

Pam and Wesley enjoyed a whirlwind courtship for several months and decided to get married. Pam had never had a 'real' wedding before and she dreamed of wearing a white gown. We went shopping together and found that the gowns you have to order were very expensive. I suggested she consider getting one that had been used at bridal shows. We found one that was pretty and fit. The only problem was that it was gray along the hem from being carried from one show to another. It was plenty long enough and I offered to re-hem it for her, which would eliminate the problem. The price was one quarter of what she would have paid for a brand new, specially ordered one.

During this pre-wedding time, my husband and I moved into a new home. I was busy making drapes, hanging pictures, painting, etc. Pam gained weight around her middle and now the gown didn't fit. I opened up the seams and with the fabric I was using to line the drapes, I inserted and attached a gusset to make the waist wider. A friend of mine owned a printing company. She printed Pam's wedding invitations at cost and I paid the bill as a partial gift. Then I planned a bridal shower. Pam and I enjoyed the entertainment of a local trio named the Jackson Brothers. I told Pam they were performing for a Sunday brunch at a nearby hotel. She fell for it and showed up to find thirteen friends and relatives waiting to surprise her. Where she and Wesley were consolidating two homes, there was little in the way of household items they would need. So I suggested everyone chip in and we presented her with a gift certificate to a bakery that made exceptional wedding cakes. The breakfast buffet was delicious and there was a lovely bouquet of flowers at her place setting. However, there was no concert by the Jackson Brothers!

Closer to the time of the wedding, the church minister wanted to meet with Pam and Wesley. They were living at Wesley's house by then and the minister (a woman) wanted to come by on a certain evening. Pam, for some reason, was uncomfortable about the visit, so she asked me to be there for moral support. It was a pleasant meeting, but I don't remember much about it except that the details of the wedding ceremony and its significance were reviewed.

It may have been a mistake on my part – but on one occasion before the plans were well underway, I asked Pam if there were a possibility of not getting married legally. My thinking was there could be some kind of ceremony where they pledged their love to each other- a ceremony that to outsiders would look like the real thing. She could have her name legally changed to Wesley's name. This way she wouldn't have to forfeit the ten thousand dollars she received as a Viet Nam military widow. "You and Wesley could enjoy the money: go on a cruise every year, buy a nice boat, etc." "No, Wesley would not go for that." Did I stick my nose out too far to suggest she not pay full price for a wedding gown, or suggest a way she might continue enjoying those government checks? Maybe so.

The wedding took place and all went well. There was a reception at a lodge not far from the church. My aunt and uncle came from South Carolina to attend and stayed at my house for a few days. My uncle was always called upon to take pictures on occasions such as these. He wasn't a professional photographer, but he might as well have been – his picture taking was that good! The morning after the wedding I hosted a brunch for out-of-town guests and some of my friends. Late morning the bride and groom appeared bringing the leftover sandwiches from the reception. That was the last time I ever saw Pam. She did send me a nice note saying I was the best matron of honor a gal ever had.

For a wedding gift I had contracted with an artist who does amazing collages. He cuts up pictures into small pieces and then reassembles them. In this case, he would take bits and pieces of the wedding pictures and put them together in such a way that from a distance, it looks like a bride cutting the cake. Up close, you see faces, hands, flowers and other recognizable items. I asked my aunt to send me a set of pictures from the wedding to get my wedding gift idea underway.

While all this was taking place, I had a suspicious mammogram and a questionable breast scan. I had had many alarms before, but I could tell by the way the technicians and other staff members were acting that this time something more serious was going on. I called Pam to see if we could get together the following Saturday so I could tell her about my situation face to face. I also wanted to escape some company I wasn't ready to deal with. Her reaction was strange. "I'll have to see if my son wants me to do anything that day."

It was said in very frosty tones. "Why do you sound so cold?" I asked. "Who said you could look at my wedding pictures? (My aunt must have told her she sent them to me because I had asked for them.) They're my pictures. You have no right to see them unless I say so." I was stunned. I couldn't think fast enough. I simply said that I now have real worries about having breast cancer and would keep her posted. We hung up. A breast biopsy did confirm I had breast cancer.

Returning home after a consultation with the surgeon, I dropped a note to Pam to let her know about the diagnosis. "Since breast cancer can run in families, be sure you and your daughter have regular mammograms." Too tired to look up Wesley's exact address, I sent it to the family home, which Pam still owned. (There is more about the breast cancer experience in Chapter 10.) That ticked her off. She called all irate. "Why did you send it to that address? You know where I live now." I asked, "Why are you being so cold toward me? What did I do to deserve this kind of treatment?" "I don't wish to go there at this time" was the answer she gave each time I asked. I had a portion of my breast removed and received anti-cancer treatments. Pam never sent me a get well card. I spoke to her daughter one time after I had been through most of the ordeal and asked her what was going on regarding her mother's attitude toward me. She said, "My mother wants distance from you." She said she didn't know any more than that. With that explanation, I replied, "OK, I'll respect that."

It saddened me to learn that Pam sold the family home to her son's sister-in-law. Where that was my grandparents' home, the home where my mother grew up and where we lived during our high school years, I was disappointed not to have been offered an opportunity to buy it myself and perhaps keep it in the immediate family. I learned about the sale after the fact. When Pam and Wesley retired they moved to Georgia. After at least five years of estrangement, she called to say I was welcome to come visit her in Georgia. My response was, "First I have to know why you turned on me when I was sick." Again, it was the same old, "I don't wish to go there at this time." "In that case don't expect me to visit."

That was how a fairly close relationship between Irish twins ended for me.

My mother asked that I keep an eye out for Pam. I tried to do my best, but I felt used and then discarded. If Pam meant to hurt me, she succeeded. I realize now that it was our mother that kept us together.

Pam was diagnosed with cancer about eight years after she married Wesley. My aunt relayed that information. She was receiving chemotherapy at the same time as my uncle who had malignant skin cancer. My aunt said that Pam wouldn't reveal where the cancer was except to say that it wasn't breast, wasn't colon and wasn't in any major organ. If it had been skin cancer, she would have shared experiences about that with my uncle. I will probably never know, but I can speculate. I passed what I knew on to Carol – the sister that Pam didn't want to call when our mother passed away – the sister who was not even invited to Pam's wedding because she disliked her so much. Low and behold, shortly after I told Carol about Pam having cancer, I received a letter from her. It said, "You'll be surprised to learn that I made plane reservations to go to Georgia to visit Pam. She talked about you a lot, showed me her wedding pictures and the counted cross stitch picture you made for her with all the different kinds of shells." Then the preaching started. "You need to remember the lessons from Mom and Dad, from church, from girl scouts, etc. and call Pam. You need to apologize for whatever she thinks you did wrong." It was a 'holier than thou' kind of message. I read it carefully and then called Carol. "I'm sure you put a lot of thought into writing that letter you sent."

"Are you going to call her, then?"

"No. I asked her many, many times what if anything I did to cause her to turn her back on me. She would never say. I left the ball in her court many years ago. I don't go around apologizing for 'whatever you think I did.'"

"Then I don't think I want you for a sister."

I had to bite my tongue...

Here was another example of Carol showing up and wanting to get involved with a family member who was terminally ill. Up until her visit to Georgia, there was absolutely no relationship between the two of them. She did this with my father and my mother. I feel certain she won't come around when I'm on the way out!

Pam gave up on the treatments and passed away about one month after Carol's visit. Carol had sent me a picture of her and Pam taken in Georgia. I hadn't seen Pam in so long that I didn't recognize her. She surely didn't look like someone who only had one month left to live. But one night, I'm told, Pam woke up in pain. She asked Wesley to give her another dose of her narcotic medication. The next time Wesley woke up Pam was dead. Of course I was sorry Pam passed away – actually, I felt a little numb about it all. At the same time, I resented that she left me to try to figure out why she 'wanted her distance' from me when I had come to her rescue so often. Was it a case of, "I have a husband now, so I don't need you?" Was it jealousy?

CAROL

Carol was born when I was four and one half years old. Her twin brother, who was also premature like Carol, did not survive. Carol must have been kept in the hospital nursery until she was mature enough to come home. I remember Aunt Annie driving Harriet, Pam and me to the hospital so my mother could bring Carol home. I don't remember a whole lot about Carol after that. Being that much younger it seemed like she was of a different generation and sometimes from a different planet. My mother had had her tubes tied after Carol and Carl, Jr. were delivered by caesarian section, so this was the last child and the baby of the family. As such, she enjoyed more privileges than Pam and I had had. For example, she was the only one who was given a car – a black VW beetle.

Growing up I thought Carol was a nuisance and quite sneaky. At Easter we each received a basket filled with lots of candy and goodies. Mother said we could only eat two pieces each day. That's what I did and hid my basket under my bed between times. One day my basket was empty and Carol was nowhere to be found. She had climbed into one of the side cupboards of the dining room buffet. We searched everywhere for her and she finally crawled out when all my candy was gone. She had chocolate all over her face and the candy wrappers were still in the cupboard. Mealtimes were often unpleasant because of Carol. We were expected to eat at least two bites of each thing on our plate before we could be excused from the table - no matter what we were served – even if it was the tough liver my grandmother cooked, we had to take two bites. Carol would not abide by the two bites rule. She would be sitting at the table long after everyone's place setting was cleared, the dishes washed, dried and put away. Still sitting there my father would argue with my mother, "You're being too hard on her."

"Why should the rule be different for her?"

Usually it all ended with Carol being sent to bed and her slamming the bedroom door on her way. Why that door never fell off its hinges is a mystery.

Once I started school, I was very involved with sports, girl scouts, church, etc. so I really don't remember much about Carol's school years. When in college, she was dating a guy who claimed to have special qualities because he was the seventh son of a seventh son. All I know was some of the children from that family (I think there were twelve) used to ride the same school bus I did. They used to come out to the bus in the morning eating their breakfasts of toast and peanut butter and looking a bit disheveled. I don't know how, when or why my sister, Carol took up with this 'seventh son' named Robert. My mother suffered another disappointment when Carol announced she was pregnant. She was in her senior year of college. Hurt, Harriet refused to attend Carol's graduation. But, she insisted that Pam and I go. Then when Carol went into labor with her first baby, Harriet came to sit with my baby, Ben. She wanted me to stay with Carol throughout her labor and delivery since obstetrical nursing was my clinical specialty.

As disappointed and hurt as she was, Harriet was trying to see that Carol had family present on these two occasions.

My grandmother (Harriet's mother) bought a baby bassinet prior to my being born. My mother used it for me, Pam, and then Carol. I'm not sure if Pam used it for any of her children, but I cleaned it up, painted it and made a nice skirt, mattress cover and pillow for it before Ben was born. Carol was due four months after Ben, so I forwarded the bassinet to her in time for the arrival of her first born. As I understand the story, Carol was wheeling the bassinet from one room to another in her apartment when it tipped going over a threshold. Robert was furious and smashed the bassinet into pieces so it couldn't ever be used again. Their baby was fine. My second child didn't get to use what I thought of as "our family bassinet."

Robert was opinioned and argumentative. When our children were babies, we would occasionally get together at my parents house on a Sunday. My mother would ask, "Giulia, please go into the living room and talk with Robert. Try to make him feel comfortable and welcome." I didn't feel like it but I did. Robert would start in with something like, "What do you think of JFK?" Whatever my answer, it would always be wrong, and he'd start arguing with me. That's why no one wanted to talk to or be with him.

There was a Sunday after Pam's husband had died and her family had moved into my parents' home when the children were playing with a beach ball in the pool. The pool was enclosed by a wooden stockade fence. That 'lighter than air' ball came over the fence and then bounced off the head of Carol's oldest son. Robert went crazy shouting that Pam's children were undisciplined, bratty and out of control. On and on he went hurling insults about her children. Hearing all this, and being protective of her fatherless grandchildren, Harriet came out of the house and gave Robert an ear full. "How dare you talk to or about Pam's children that way? They live here; they are welcome here – you are not. Don't ever come here again. Those children have lost their father. They are well behaved and dearly loved." Thereafter, I suspect Carol could only come to visit when Robert gave her permission. Of course, Carl and Harriet were no longer welcome in Robert's house either. When Carol did show up, it was often in the middle of Sunday dinner. Trying to be welcoming and polite, Harriet would attempt to make space for four more additional people at the table. So we all moved this way and that to make room for Carol's family (sans Robert) and then sat down to a meal that had by that time grown cold. Carol couldn't see the inconvenience she was causing nor the extra work she was making for Harriet. Couldn't she have offered to wait in the living room until the meal was over or plan her arrival earlier or later?

I'm told that Carol was an excellent and dedicated counselor to groups of mentally challenged children. She was devoted to each one of them and personally thrilled when they made the slightest progress. At the end of a school year, there would be a 'show and tell' type of program so the children could proudly demonstrate what they had accomplished. Carol invited my parents to attend one of those programs. Robert got wind of the plans and was in the school's parking lot when Harriet and Carl arrived. He chased their car all around the grounds shouting, "I know your dirty little secret." There was no way they could get out of the car without the risk of being hit. My father later told me, "We were like lambs being led to the slaughter." I couldn't imagine what the 'dirty little secret' was. Harriet and Carl returned home and never saw the performance.

Moving forward several years, my daughter was working as a manager of a coffee shop when Carol happened to stop in to meet a friend. My daughter thought she recognized her and initiated a conversation about where she was living, how her children were, etc. I followed up on the details of their conversation and realized she and Robert were living at different addresses. With Robert out of the picture, I decided it might be safe to call and possibly plan a get-together. In total, I believe we had one meeting and half a dozen phone conversations. I was dismayed to learn of all the resentments she harbored and emotional baggage she carried.

Carl never should have done it, but he once told Pam that when my mother was pregnant and found she was carrying twins, she became a 'basket case.' She had a four year old, a three year old and couldn't imagine being able to manage twins, too. She was going nuts. She said to my father, "Step on me. Jump on me. Do something. I can't go through with this." Of course, there was nothing Carl could do. When Carol was still in the hospital with her first born, Pam told her that story. Why did she do that? To this day, Carol believes her mother tried to murder her and probably caused her twin brother's death. As mentioned previously, Carl, Jr. died of immature lungs due to prematurity – not from fetal or uterine trauma. Carol told Robert her beliefs on this matter and that's what was behind Robert's accusations of, "I know your dirty little secret." I asked Carol if she knew Robert occasionally called Harriet and Carl in the middle of the night to make similar remarks. (He worked the night shift.) She said she didn't know about that. She admitted he was difficult but she stayed with him until he finally earned a college degree. By that time, her children were grown and had children of their own.

Another resentment she still holds is that her children didn't get to carry Harriet's coffin. That matter was presented earlier.

At some point when we met, the matter of Carol and I not being very close to her came up. I explained that as for me, her husband was the reason. Frankly, I wasn't certain of his stability and was somewhat afraid of him. She stated, "Even if he were a murderer, I was still your sister." I never asked, but I wonder what it was she expected any of us were supposed to do given her modus operandi: coming around unpredictably and not very often. Even when Harriet's mother died, she didn't come to the funeral. Harriet delayed the service as long as she could hoping Carol would attend. But she didn't. It isn't funny, but Carol said to me, "You know, Grandma always said I was her favorite."

Her list of complaints about me, Pam and Harriet was lengthy- too many complaints to remember. I did have the thought that she was carrying too much of an emotional burden and perhaps some counseling would help. I couldn't bring myself to say that, for fear of her reaction. She was, after all, righteous and I was not. Robert's behaviors were bizarre, but Carol's were strange, tool.

When I didn't respond to Carol's order to call Pam and apologize for 'whatever she thinks you did,' she denounced me as a sister. I'm sorry to admit it, but there was no sense of loss for me. You can't lose what you never had.

ANOTHER CARL

A baby brother at age seventy-one?
How did that happen?

After my father passed away, I decided it was about time I told my mother that I was separated from my husband and initiating divorce. She had been very fond of him because of his boyish and fun-loving ways and because he did lots of big and small repairs around her house. It was planned we should meet around lunch time on a Saturday at Harriet's house. Pam said she'd come by in case I needed moral support. The discussion began and as expected, my mother was disappointed to hear my news. I explained my version of why I was unhappy being married to Charlie and interestingly, Pam added a few examples I hadn't thought of. Then Pam, I guess to direct the focus away from my story, told some unpleasant details of the problems her daughter had gotten into. Pam explained that I had been a big help getting her daughter's situation taken care of. Then my mother said, "Well as long as we're having a session of true confessions, I have a story to tell."

Apparently, when I was in fifth or sixth grade, my father left our family for a while. I never knew why and I am not certain it was the first time. What I learned from my mother's story was that Carl had had an affair with a much younger woman who rode on his bus. She got pregnant and had a baby boy she named Carl after my father. Somehow my mother figured out what was going on.

One day, on her lunch hour, she was in a department store that was running a beautiful baby picture contest. There she saw a picture of baby Carl that looked just like Carol's baby pictures. Harriet confronted Carl, "If you confess, I will never bring it up to you ever again. If you don't, I will make the rest of your life miserable." So he confessed.

Next, my mother went to visit baby Carl's mother, who lived with her mother. Essentially, her message to these two women was, "If you persist in being in my husband's life, we will sue you for custody of the baby." Harriet also told us that she asked the grandmother, "Do you think it's right of your daughter to take a father away from his three girls?" As far as I know, Carl never had any further contact with his son's mother.

It was a heavy session we had that day. I was dealing with my own issues of divorce and after that was helping my mother with her series of health problems. I only had a last name associated with this baby Carl to go on and with a lapse of time was not certain of that. Harriet explained that she revealed this information in case Carl's son should 'come out of the woodwork' after she was gone to claim some share of the estate. That didn't happen.

Pam and I made at least one half-hearted attempt to at least find where this new Carl lived. I think we were in the right town, but somehow the street we were looking for ended where a shopping mall had been built. We gave up the search and went shopping at the mall instead.

I didn't start looking again for Carl for several years. Interest in my genealogy peaked an interest in searching for my own half-brother again. His birth year was unknown to me as was his mother's name. The mistaken date I had guessed at produced two men who had lived in the town where my father Carl had driven his bus. I wrote to each of them asking if they might be the missing person I was looking for. Both called me and clearly they were not the ones. But I said, "You sound very nice. I wish you were the brother I've been looking for." My friend Ella and I made some visits to the town halls where we thought he might have lived to look through records. Again, I didn't have any accurate dates and being an illegitimate child, useful records wouldn't have been open to us anyway. I quizzed my aunt several times to see what she could remember about my father's son. She only knew there was a baby and his name was Carl, but nothing more. My uncle said the family name I had sounded right.

It was a fluke that one day I typed in the name I thought was the one—and up came an obituary notice in which the name I had was listed as a step-son of the deceased. It also listed the name of the man's wife. When I typed in that name, I discovered that this woman passed away only one month earlier and it listed the name of a son – Carl. I began to believe that this could be my half-brother. I was only off regarding birth dates by ten years. This time I wrote the following note:

> "I am sorry to learn that your mother has passed away. When I read her obituary, I wondered if you might be the half-brother I have been searching for. Did your mother ever work at McMahon's Restaurant when she was young and did she ever live in Sussex? Here is my number. Please call. Let me know either way if you might be who I'm looking for."

I mailed the letter on a Friday afternoon. On Monday evening a man called stating he had received my note and asked, "What was your maiden name?" I told him. He said, "Then I am the one you are looking for." I was so amazed and stunned that I remember little of the rest of the conversation. Up until then, it was as if I were looking for an inanimate object – now that name was a real person with a voice and a memory. It was a peculiar feeling. I had to pinch myself over and over again to determine that all this was now real. I had opened up a door and wondered where it would lead. My new brother, Carl, and I decided to meet for coffee. For over two and a half hours we sat in a coffee shop exchanging pictures and sharing personal family stories regarding our parents and our upbringing. It pleased me so much to discover I had a brother who was handsome, hardworking, polite and interesting. Carl has been a letter carrier for many years. The weight of all those magazines, etc. he's been delivering has taken a toll on the nerves and muscles of his neck and back. He's close to retirement now, and I hope he can get there without further harm/pain. In retirement years, he'll be able to more fully enjoy his hobby – model trains. He has no regrets about his childhood. He said, "I didn't have everything there was, but I didn't go without." Family members paid for him to attend parochial school. On occasion, he asked his mother if he had had a father. Her answer was, "Yes, you did, but he's not around anymore."

Carl was apparently content with that explanation, but his wife insisted on learning more. She quizzed Carl's aunt who was thirteen years older than Carl's mother and the aunt 'spilled the beans,' according to Carl. After the death of either his mother or his aunt, Carl came across my father's obituary and a newspaper article about his driving the bus for over fifty years. That is how Carl learned he had three half sisters. He said, "I knew there were three of you, but I didn't know if you knew anything about me. I decided not to contact you because I didn't want to alarm or upset you."

It's curious how closely our paths have crossed. For example, he once worked for a catalogue store owned by a man named Sid. I babysat for Sid's children all through high school. Of course these events didn't occur simultaneously because Carl was so much younger than I was. After high school, Carl enrolled in the local university to study accounting because that's what some of his friends were doing. Going to college didn't appeal to Carl, so he dropped out after two years. That following September was when I came on the faculty at that university.

We plan future get-togethers with other members of our families. Carl has a daughter who is engaged to be married and a son with two children. I look forward to those meetings.

My aunt asked, "How do you think your mother would feel if she knew you had made contact with this fellow?" "She probably wouldn't like it, but anyone—including my mother—would be pleased to know that this baby turned out so fine." Other friends have asked how I feel about my father having had an affair. I have no idea why he did that, but he was a good father to me. He loved me unconditionally. That's what is and was important to me.

My regret is that I couldn't have known my brother, Carl, sooner.

CHAPTER 3

School Years

In the early forties there was no preschool or preprimary in the city where I lived. The year you turned five was the year you started first grade. There was no better introduction to the beaucoup years of education ahead than to have Mrs. Bates for a first grade teacher. She was like a grandmother: round both of body and face. She had short, gray permed hair, rosy cheeks and a twinkle in her eye. She let you hug her if you wished.

We learned to print manuscript letters in first grade. Mrs. Bates gave each of us a sheet of math paper with an uppercase and lowercase letter on it. We would place that paper on a felt board and with a stylus that had a sharp pin sticking out of it, we would prick the shape of the letters. Then, when the job was well done, she would clip each child's paper with tiny, tiny metal pins (like miniature clothes pins with little pointy hooks on the back) and hang them on wires all around the room.

Until first grade I always colored in coloring books. I was proud of how I stayed inside the lines and of how I kept my crayons pointy. I colored each page in order. "Can't wait to color page 4, but I have to do pages 1, 2 and 3 first!" One fall day the class went for a walk – two abreast and holding hands. Mrs. Bates picked a sprig of goldenrod and back in the classroom we were instructed to draw the goldenrod on a blank piece of paper. This was my first attempt at purposeful, freehand drawing. I took a green crayon and drew a stem with branches coming off of it. Then I took a yellow crayon and pounded yellow all over the green lines. It was a work of art, of course, and it ended up being clipped and displayed on those classroom wires.

First grade was a joyful experience. I loved recess: jump rope, hopscotch, "A my name is Alice," jacks and marbles. But there was one incident that mars my first grade memories. It was time to go home on a cold Friday before Christmas vacation. In the seasonal excitement, I failed to heed the visceral calling of my bowels. Somewhere between the classroom and the coatroom, something dreadful happened. Mrs. Bates traced the unpleasant odor to me and gently asked if I had had an accident. I objected so vehemently and tearfully, that she didn't have the heart to pursue the matter. I just wanted to make a fast getaway. Oh how I wish I had had the courage to admit to my shortcoming. I probably wouldn't have had to walk all the way home with poops going down my legs and soaking into my woolen leggings.

As the older of Irish twin sisters I suffered from an obsession to be perfect. Thus, as a student, my behaviors would, no doubt, classify me as a "teacher's pet." Miss Grump was my second grade teacher. She was old, had dull, yellowish, gray hair on her head and long hairs growing out of her face. During reading exercises, she would place a chair in front of the classroom beside her for me to sit in. Handing me a pair of tweezers she would say, "Giulia, please pluck out the hairs on my chin." While the other students took turns stumbling through the readings, I plucked away. At the end of the reading session, Miss Grump would open her purse and give me a nickel. I sensed this was crazy, but I always did what I was told and I did love money.

There were also times when Miss Grump would need to leave the room. Again, she would have me sit in front of the classroom with a paper and pencil. "Write down the names of anyone who misbehaves," she instructed me. When anyone did act up I would say something like, "Stop doing that or I will write down your name!" When she returned, I received another nickel. You would think that the other kids would have hated me. If they did, I never knew it. Furthermore, I didn't feel I should tell my mother and cause her to get upset. My sister didn't tell because with the nickels Miss Grump gave me, I would stop at the corner store on the way home and buy hard tack candy for the two of us. I realize now that Miss Grump was leaving the room to smoke a cigarette. At the time, I thought she needed to use the ladies room. Her smoking probably accounts for why her hair was such an ugly yellow. Incidentally, my report card shows a "B" in reading for second grade. Perhaps if I had read more and plucked less, I would have had an "A."

I started in a new school for fourth grade because my parents had purchased a bungalow adjacent to an affluent community. No one could beat me at running; no one in the whole school – boy or girl. There were semi-organized races at recess and I won almost all of the time. One day a boy named Jeff tried to slow me down by grabbing the belt on the back of my coat. He tore off the belt, the buttons and two chunks of fabric where the buttons were sewn on. I was furious, turned on him and pummeled him to the ground. The two of us had to stay for detention – he for damaging another's property and me for using my fists instead of words. That evening, Jeff's mother called our home and offered to have the coat repaired. (Where Jeff's father was in the coat manufacturing business, they could well afford to supply a new coat.) But my mother said, "No thanks, I'll fix it myself." She was just as angry as I was.. I think she would have pummeled him herself if she had been there.

It is embarrassing to recall, but fifth grade is where I learned to cheat. Maybe it was because I was used to being at the top of my class in previous grades. Now except for recess, I was facing a lot of academic competition. Miss Kennedy had a "100 Club." At the end of each month we would count up the number of 100s we had earned. One boy and one girl were declared winners and entitled to special privileges. I have no recollection of what those privileges were – couldn't have been extraordinary. Miss Kennedy kept track of the test and papers she graded, but she gave pop quizzes that fellow students corrected. If you received 100% on those tests, you could cut up a slip of paper, mark it with your name and "100" and save it to count up at the end of the month. So I made up 100% slips of paper for myself and stacked them up inside my desk to be sure I would win each month. Surely Miss Kennedy knew. Some months I probably had more 100% slips than there had been quizzes. Why didn't she say something? I'm embarrassed about doing that, not because it was wrong, but because she knew and didn't say anything.

There was a big fire during the summer between fifth and sixth grade. A nearby elementary school burned to the ground. The city's school board distributed all the students among several other schools. Our two sixth grade classes were transferred to sub-basement rooms in the Junior High School. The teacher, Mrs. Burton had many geranium plants along a wall counter. Those plants had to reach so high up to get some light that they ended up looking like elephant ears on spindly legs. Girls were scheduled to take home economics (cooking and sewing) in seventh grade and therefore sewed aprons during sixth grade. The apron pieces were cut from stiff muslin and not easy to penetrate with a needle. Nevertheless, we had to make narrow, little hem stitches all around the outside edges. Next, we attached a pocket again with tiny stitches and made a loop that would attach to a dishcloth. Finally, we embroidered our names on the bib section. The sewing teacher was annoyed with me. She said my hands were sweaty and I was rusting too many needles. I took home a note from her saying I needed to bring in a powder puff to keep my hands dry. Up until then, I had done quite a lot of sewing and needlework on my own. My friend Carolyn and I used to sew doll clothes by the hour. Frankly, I think the sewing teacher disliked me because I sewed just as well as she did – maybe even better.

One of my classmates in sixth grade had a neat trick. During a test, she would have answers written on a crib sheet. At a convenient time, she would make herself throw up and run to the girls' room where she could double check her answers. I don't think the rest of us knew how to throw up spontaneously—but wouldn't that have been a scene if we were all throwing up and running around?

I don't have a positive memory of my sixth grade teacher. Making conversation with her one day at recess, I told her I was planning to go to college. (I probably didn't even know what college was, but it sounded good to me.) She asked, "How in the world are YOU ever going to college?" I said I would get scholarships. Her reply was a snide, "YOU get a scholarship?" I thought of that conversation the day I earned a Doctorate Degree from a major university. Almost all of my undergraduate and graduate education was covered by scholarships. She was mean. She misjudged me!

We didn't have to go far for seventh grade. We were still in the basement of the Junior High, but on an opposite side of the building from where we were for sixth grade. In fact, my homeroom was in the print shop where, for a one-half a term, the boys were introduced to the trade skills of graphics. Students in that homeroom had to climb over the foot pedals of the presses and when a big printing project was in progress, we had to be careful moving around for fear of getting some ink on our clothes. At Christmas time someone proposed that we exchange presents. We each picked out the name of someone else in the class to buy a 25-cent present for. One boy named Bud checked around to find out who had my name and he exchanged names with that person. When the gift exchange took place I opened a gift that cost more than 25 cents. It was a metal, gold-colored, case that, when opened up, held folding picture pockets to hold 20 2×2 photos. Of course, he had placed his own picture inside. I was embarrassed to receive this present. I didn't want a boyfriend and was uncomfortable to receive something better than what others got. At that tender age I felt I had to ignore or deny his infatuation with me. He became a renowned surgeon and a successful and honorable man. I'm 99% certain he remembers nothing of the above incident. Anyway, I filled the photo case with pictures and kept it for a long, long time.

Miss Wilson in 8th grade was my all-time favorite teacher. If one could call up an image of an aging, single school marm, one would have a fairly clear picture of Miss Wilson. Somehow I sensed it really mattered to her that we should learn. My seat was in the second row, third seat in. It's as if I were sitting there just yesterday. She taught English and history and genuinely loved her subject matter. In particular, she made parsing paragraphs fun. Every word in a sentence, no matter how complicated or how long had a special place when it was diagrammed. I don't think many students are taught that today. Ask a roomful of people what a gerund phrase[6] is, and I doubt many will know. I realized that when I studied some foreign languages. Some of the students had difficulty composing because they never learned what gerunds were or other more basic parts of speech. One morning a professor asked a student to state in the language we were studying why she was late for class. What she tried to say was that the apartment's toilet was clogged. When she looked up "clog" she took the noun meaning shoe instead of the verb "to clog." What she ended up was a mishmash of a sentence saying something about a shoe and a toilet. Thank you Miss Wilson for giving me a "leg up" about a language's grammatical construction.

Miss Wilson would often offer us a challenge such as "Find out why Connecticut is called the Nutmeg State."[7] Then she would say, "Dollars to donuts no one will search for the answer." That was the kind of stimulation I responded to. I went through the *Information Please Almanac* my parents gave me each Christmas and any other references I had access to until I found an answer. At

---

6   A gerund is a verb that ends in *-ing* and functions as a noun which expresses action or a state of being.

7   Connecticut was called the Nutmeg State because Yankee peddlers would sell small carved knobs of wood shaped like a nutmeg to the Native Americans and to other unsuspecting customers.

first, Miss Wilson was surprised that I could come up with a reply, but eventually, she knew she would hear from me when she issued a challenge. What she didn't know was how happy I was to spend time at my desk searching for information. That desk was without a doubt the best Christmas present I ever received. I know now that it was defective and probably on clearance because one of the legs wouldn't screw into the bottom properly. But once it was glued or nailed in place, I sat at that desk by the hour reading Nancy Drew mysteries and keeping myself busy with writing letters to cousins and pen pals and doing homework.

Miss Calomine was the school nurse. She smelled like soap. She came to each 8th grade classroom regularly to teach hygiene and nutrition. Her topic one day was dental care. She asked who knew something about preventing tooth decay. Kevin, who never spoke or raised his hand, was excited because he said he knew the answer. Miss Calomine called on him. "Chew Dentyne gum," he said. Miss Calomine put on an incredulous look that was a signal for us all to laugh. The poor guy must have felt like a fool. I'd like to see Kevin today. He probably has perfect teeth while most of the rest of us have fillings, crowns, bridges and root canals. Eighth grade is a little late to learn about tooth brushing. (Fluoride and flossing wasn't in the repertoire of dental care at that time.) Furthermore, what were we to do about facts on nutrition? We ate what our parents served. AMEN.

By eighth grade I had begun to fancy that I might have a future as a teacher of home economics in spite of the critical sewing teacher I had had in sixth grade. The home economics schedule called for a half year of cooking and a half year of sewing – all on the 3rd floor of the building. Meanwhile the boys were in the basement taking graphics and mechanical drawing. Early in the school year, in cooking class, we made oatmeal or porridge. It was yucky and we didn't want to eat it. Although I did not see it myself, one girl opened the window and dumped her pan of porridge below. Unfortunately, on the ground level was the parking area for the teachers and administrators. The porridge landed on the roof of the principal's car. It wasn't until the end of the day, when he was leaving for home that the sticky mess was discovered. By then, it was too late to figure out who or which class had created such a porridge avalanche. Perhaps if the principal had investigated which girl did not have a stomach ache that day, he would have had a clue.

Sewing class was a total disappointment. Since by then, I had done lots of sewing and needlework, the jumper with straight seams we all had to make was terribly boring. At the end of the year there was to be a fashion show with each of us walking out across the stage wearing the same dress. Now that was real fashion! Unfortunately, I moved through the sewing project too quickly, so Mrs. Pleat decided to undo all my stitching. She said, "You're too far ahead of the other students, so you can start over." I never wished to be a home economics teacher after that.

During the same year, I experienced a throbbing pain in my foot. It was a plantar wart and walking one and a half miles each way to and from school drove the wart deep into my foot. The Podiatrist arranged for me to have x-ray therapy at a local hospital to kill the virus causing the wart. It took three treatments for it to dry up and fall out. It looked like a wrinkled piece of corn. I had to be dismissed from school early on the three Thursdays when my treatments took place. One day I was supposed to go to a different hospital to visit my younger cousin who was a patient there. Our class had done poorly on a test that day. Miss Wilson decided to keep us all after school to review the questions and answers one by one. I got very nervous with this unexpected development because I knew my aunt would be waiting for me. I raised my hand to explain my dilemma. However, Miss Wilson was so frustrated with the class that she said, "Put your hand down. It'll be your turn to speak when I get to you." So desk by desk, she went around the room. All the while, I'm squirming and sweating. Finally, when she got to me, I shouted out, "But, I was supposed to be at the hospital a half hour ago!" Of course she assumed I was expected at the hospital for another treatment. She quickly helped me get my stuff together so I could leave. That night she called my mother. "I am so sorry. Never should I have kept Giulia after school. She's the only one who had a passing grade. I will never do that again. Please tell Giulia that I was wrong and I am sorry."

Why are my memories of eighth grade so clear to me? Why is that eight grade should be so fresh in my mind? For one thing, I think educational specialists would say that I had arrived at a state of learning readiness. I began to attach personal meaning to and internalize what we were studying. For example, I wondered what kind of life I would have had, had I lived in one of those early American colonies. Would I have been a seamstress making wide dresses with lots of petticoats? Maybe I might have been a milliner. My learning readiness was no doubt enhanced my Miss Wilson's challenging teaching style. Whatever the reason, everything that went into my head stayed there. I became a lover of learning. Miss Wilson and I stayed in touch off and on for many years. Once, when my children were school age, I invited her to my home for Sunday dinner. I told her how wonderful she looked. She replied, "A little powder and a little paint makes you look like what you ain't." After dinner, she engaged the attention of my children and had them parsing sentences!

Onto ninth grade we went. It was the last year we would spend at the Junior High School. I was elected president of my homeroom. My big undertaking that year was to plan a field trip to an historical seaport. The bus we needed required twice the number of passengers than we had in our class. So I arranged for my sister's homeroom class to join us. I made a pretty dress to wear: pink, gray and white with inch wide shoulder straps. It was a Friday before Memorial Day weekend and everything was per-fect including the weather. I ended up with the worst sunburn of my life. You could see where my dress straps had been many weeks later. At the end of ninth grade, there was a school prom. My mother and I made lovely, lavender, brocaded dress. A boy named Brett was my date. His father was an elderly, old-fashioned man who drove an antique car he called "the box." Brett and I were childhood chums. We had spent some time designing a plan where with certain clues we would astonish other kids with our psychic powers, guessing which card the person had picked. After the card was picked, I would phone Brett. If I asked, "What suit do we have here?" He would know it was a spade. If I asked, "Can you sense what suit this is?" He would know it was a diamond. Then I would start with another set of clues. "What is the card I have in my hand?" He would then look down a long list of clues to figure it was a 10. It took a bit of time for us to devise this game – but it took even longer for us to pull off the right answer. I doubt anyone believed that we had psychic powers. But we thought we were quite clever!

We probably didn't dance much at the prom. However, afterwards the "box" took us to an amusement park. There in my lavender, very feminine prom dress, I rode the roller coaster over and over screaming my head off. Then we went on the Ferris wheel and tilt-a-whirl. There was nothing feminine about my running from one wild ride to another with skirts flying in the breeze. I met Brett at a 50th high school reunion. He remembered going to the prom in the "box" but nothing else. How could he forget?

Off then to a very large city high school. When we graduated, there were 620 in the class. The main building of the school was a large, old, ornate, building with a beautiful clock tower above that could be seen for miles around. The study hall was on the top floor, divided into four quadrants with about fifty desks in each section. Hanging from the ceiling were large, bowl-shaped lamps. Quite often some of the boys (never the girls!) would try to throw coins up and into the lamps. That caused some distracting pinging noises. Then there would be an investigation about where the coins came from. It was hard to get much studying done in study hall with 200 students and lots of commotion. The school had state championship basketball teams year after year. The players had a large basketball court to play on. I never went into the boys' locker room, but I'm quite certain there were showers there. However, that was not the case for the girls who played varsity basketball. Our basketball court was on the top of the oldest part of the building and the lockers were on the floor below with no showers. Having made it on the varsity team in my junior year, I reported to the gym every morning as required by the coach, put on my gym clothes, did my workout exercises, worked up a sweat and then put my school clothes back on and went to class. The team members repeated all those steps after school when we didn't have a game and then went home on the late bus. Most of the schools we played against did have showers and nice accommodations. Somehow our lack of facilities didn't really concern me. I just wanted to play my heart out and win. Back then, girls didn't run the whole court. Guards would steal/capture/rebound the ball from the forwards of the other team, dribble it to half court and pass it to one of our own forwards who would then hopefully make the moves to get us a basket. Some said I played "dirty." I could anticipate where the ball was going but pretend I was looking the other way. But then, like a viper, I would strike to grab the ball or steal it. Also, if one of the other team's forwards started to dribble toward the basket, I would plant myself in the way and then fall down making it look like she had "charged" into me. That would give one of our forwards a chance to shoot for a 2-point basket. Miss Snow, our coach, knew what I was doing and I could see she was shaking her head and chuckling on the sidelines. At half time, the host school would serve orange wedges on a tray. For a sweaty, exhausted body those oranges were incredibly delicious. Our uniforms were cumbersome outfits: a skirted jumper with a white blouse underneath. I was awarded an athletic scholarship to college because of playing my heart out for our varsity team.

I took the usual college prep courses. Geometry was particularly enjoyable. Finding the degree of an unknown angle of a polygon was like detective work. Today, I am disappointed about what I didn't learn in algebra. Never was it made clear that algebraic formulas could be represented by a graph: Y goes here and X goes there. How much more I might have learned had I appreciated that connection. Graphing formulas would again have been like detective work for me.

Maintaining a B or above in my entire course work entitled me to automatic entry to a state college without taking entrance exams. That made senior year a little less stressful than it might have been. I was elected editor of the class's yearbook. With 620 graduates, it was a big undertaking. However, I had an experienced faculty advisor. We didn't deviate much from previous years' formats and I surrounded myself with bright and competent assistants who then made me look capable and successful. That strategy has served me well in many subsequent undertakings.

All my running around and participating in so many activities was well rewarded at graduation time. In addition to the athletic scholarship, I received an Adaskin Foundation Scholarship, the Jewish War Veterans Brotherhood Award, the Daughters' of the American Revolution Award and a Fradkin Scholarship. In addition, my classmates voted me Best Speaker, Best All Around Student and Most Likely to Succeed. I left high school on a high note except for one thing. The guy I would have liked to go to the prom with was too shy to ask me. He finally got up the courage after I accepted (at the last minute) an invitation from someone else. My date thought of himself as a Big Man on Campus (BMOC). He wasn't in my eyes and it was unfortunately a boring evening. Most couples at the prom had an automatic date to go to the beach the next day. Not me – I never heard from him again. Perhaps it was because he tried to go "too far" and I rebuffed his advances. *C'est la vie.*

The guy I preferred to go to the prom with never went. He sent me a bouquet of flowers on Class Day. I still have the note he sent with the flowers: To Giulia, With Love, Tom.

CHAPTER 4

On My Honor

Next to my mother, no one or nothing had more of an influence on my life, my values, my problem solving and my desire to make the best of every situation than girl scouting.

In Girl Scouts, you can sing loud and off-key and no one cares – no one says, "Just move your lips, please." Being a Brownie was the first level of scouting available to me and I joined a troop as soon as I was seven. I loved being a Brownie and I sang with much gusto:

> "I have something in my pocket
> That belongs upon my face.
> I keep it very close at hand
> in a most convenient place.
> I know you'd never guess it
> if it takes a long, long time,
> So, I'll take it out and put it on.
> It's a great big Brownie smile.
> (Big Smile)"

Enchanting is what being a Brownie Girl Scout was for me. I fell for the fairy tale-like brownie story hook, line and sinker.

Two girls lived in a cottage at the edge of the forest with their elderly parents who worked their fingers to the bone every day. Often they would wish that the brownies would come to help out with household chores. The girls decided to ask the wise-old owl where they could find some brownies. The owl answered that there were two brownies living right in their own home. "Where can we find them?" one of the girls asked. He told the girls to go to the pond in the magic forest, turn around three times and say, "Twist me and turn me and show me the elf....I looked in the water and saw _____." When you finish the rhyme, you will see the brownie (s) in the pond.

When they discovered **they** were the brownies the owl reminded them, "You must be ready to help those around you, make friends and every day try to discover something new." At home they began to clean the house. In the morning, the elderly parents asked, "Who did this?" The girls danced around shouting, "It's the brownies." Thereafter, theirs was a happy little house because of the brownies.

We would enact that story about once a month. The troop leader would twist us and turn us and we would look into a mirror she had placed on the floor and happily shout, "And saw myself." She would ask what good deeds we had done. My mother was a Brownie leader's assistant, so she knew all about the story and a Brownie's promise to help others. Occasionally, Pam and I would get inspired, do some cleaning around the house and then hide. Harriet would play along. "Oh look, the

Brownies have been here. How wonderful. I hope they come again." Pam and I were fulfilling the Brownie promise when we did these good deeds:

> On my honor, I will try
> to do my duty to God and country,
> to help other people at all times,
> especially those at home.

It's funny, but for all the times I recited that promise, I never realized "especially those at home" meant the people you lived with. I always thought it meant unfortunate folks who live in an orphans home or invalids confined to a nursing home.

I wore my Brownie uniform, beanie and pin with pride – it gave me a feeling of camaraderie and of belonging to something large even though I didn't comprehend yet what world-wide meant. I did understand that the ceremonies and rituals we enacted were being done by other Brownies far and wide. Besides singing, we did crafts, took nature walks and played Brownie games such as lemme sticks.

Brownie scouting was for girls aged seven to nine. After those two years, there was a 'fly-up' ceremony. A small wooden bridge was placed on the floor. The Brownie leader said something nice like, "You are about to become a Junior Girl Scout. I give you your Brownie wings so you may fly to bigger things." She would pin a badge of yellow wings on our uniform. Then the Junior Girl Scout leader would ask us to cross the bridge one at a time and attach the Junior Scout pin to our uniform. We would stand in a horseshoe circle with other members of the Junior troop and sing:

> Make new friends,
> but keep the old.
> One is silver and the
> other gold.

In my second year of being a Brownie, I went to an overnight Girl Scout camp. Being the youngest campers there, we slept in a wooden bunkhouse. I was in a top bunk, which is what I wanted. There was a bit of a problem when you needed to go to the john at night. The john was outside, about fifty yards from the far end of the bunkhouse. I needed to be careful not to disturb the girl in the lower bunk when climbing down. One night I felt an urgent call to get to the john quickly. I probably drank too much lemonade at the evening campfire. I got myself out of the bunk and onto the floor and hurried along between all the bunks to the back door. The door was locked. The exit at the other end of the bunkhouse required one to go through or by the leader's quarters and the nurse's office. The last thing I wanted to do was disturb adults. So I squatted down far away from my own bunk and peed on the floor. It was a huge puddle and was still there in the morning. That caused a commotion. "Who did this?" No one answered. Everyone probably thought it must have been one of the girls in the bunks next to the puddle. It was far, far away from my bunk bed! Honesty wasn't in the Girl Scout promise!

That first year I went to overnight camp, it was only for one week. My sister and I were the talk of the camp for the way my mother had packed our clothes. All our outfits (shorts, jerseys, undies and socks) were in sets labeled with the days of the week on them. She didn't want us to wear mismatched clothes. Except for the 'formal days' when you had to wear the camp uniform, who really cared whether you were coordinated or not?

What I enjoyed most about camp was canteen, swimming, campfires, making gimp lanyards and eating in the mess hall. I disliked horseback riding. Sergeant was really a nice, gentle and old horse – but he was so high up and wanted to eat leaves off the trees when I was on him. I was supposed to be in control and stop him from grazing, but all I could think of was, "How much longer do I have to be up here? Hurry up Sergeant and let's get this over with." I tried hard not to look scared.

When our family moved to a different section of the city, we joined a Junior Girl Scout troop led by Mrs. Ray. She was ambitious for us and for herself. We earned many badges and Mrs. Ray made sure we met all the requirements. My badge sash was so full, the head of the Girl Scout council once told my mother, "When Giulia has breasts, she'll need a brass bra to hold up that sash." (See Appendix C.)

Mrs. Ray continued as our leader when we became Senior Scouts. Every spring we went off camping. For example, we camped somewhere in the Appalachians on our way to Arlington, Virginia so we could tour all the Washington D.C. Monuments and famous homes. Mrs. Ray envisioned our troop spending a summer camping and touring Europe. The Girl Scout organization prohibits receiving contributions- all money in the troop's treasury had to be earned. Since many of us were not yet sixteen, we took on any money raising project we could get. We planned children's birthday parties, ran dances, washed combs and brushes in beauty parlors, babysat, sold cookies, peanuts and calendars and stored newspapers in Mrs. Ray's garage to sell to a junk dealer.

While this enormous 'Europe or bust' project was underway, we learned that the first International Girl Scout and Girl Guide Roundup was going to take place in Pontiac, Michigan. (A Roundup is equivalent to the Jamboree available for Boy Scouts.) Each council could send one troop of eight girls.) Our council encompassed one city and seven surrounding towns. Training sessions were held that focused on camping and survival skills. Then there was the "try out" weekend where judges evaluated us individually, on everything we did or didn't do. I never saw the evaluation sheet, but I suspect it included such things as:

- how quickly can she make a campfire that will boil water?
- did she wear weather-appropriate clothing?
- does she participate in singing and storytelling?
- can she lash and tie appropriate knots?
- does she help others?

Shortly after, a letter arrived. I had been selected to go and, scoring the most points, would also be the patrol leader. Thereafter the eight of us and two alternates went camping once a month to continue building up our skills and an esprit-de-corps. We went to places where there was nothing but woods or a field. We lashed sticks together over a hole in the ground to make a sit down toilet, built elevated fireplaces for cooking and lashed the equivalent of kitchen counters where we washed and dried our dishes as well as ourselves. We pitched our tents and dug deep holes in the ground to keep our food cool. It was satisfying to be so independent of worldly goods and yet be dependent on each other to be successful at this scouting adventure.

I remember only one unfortunate episode. Ann woke up screaming one night because of a terribly loud buzzing in her ear. There was always an adult assigned to be nearby on these camping sessions. We took Ann to her. First, she shone a flashlight in her ear thinking it could be a bug that might move toward the light and come out. She could see a bug, but it was stuck. She then poured rubbing alcohol in Ann's ear to drown the critter. That stopped the buzzing. The next morning, Ann was taken to an emergency room where the bug was removed and put in a jar for Ann to keep. It was a Japanese beetle.

Finally, the time came to go to the Roundup. Our tents and gear were packed into wooded crates and put on a train leaving from the nearest big city station headed for Michigan. Because of the council's limited funds, the eight of us wearing ID dog tags were put in the coach section of that same train. It was exciting at first. We boarded on a Saturday morning and sat or stood up in the aisle all day. We tried to sleep at night sitting in those upright crowded seats – but most of us could only doze. There was clutter everywhere; our clothes were hanging from the shelves above and our belongings were crowded all around us. Arriving in Michigan the next day, I became motion sick as soon as I stepped onto the unmoving platform. My senses had adapted to the motion of the train and the sudden lack of movement upset my equilibrium. I stumbled around and held onto my fellow troop members until I got my bearings. The army was waiting for the thousands of campers who were all arriving that day to participate in the first International Girl Scout Roundup. They transported us and our trunks via caravans to assigned, marked campsites. It was a square plot of land in a meadow surrounded by campsites of girls from other states and countries. Next to us were Girl Scouts from Texas and Maryland. There was plenty of space between each campsite for privacy.

The army had set up a tripod with a lister bag hanging from it, which they filled with drinking water every day. This would be our home for a week. We organized our site just as we had before with a hidden toilet, kitchen area and a nice elevated fireplace for cooking and campfires. There were lots of activities planned for us including an evening in a large amphitheater with Charlton Heston as the key note speaker. Never having been a movie buff, I didn't really appreciate who he was or what he said; for sure he had wonderful things to say about girl scouting. What I do remember though was the original Roundup song we were taught and sang in rounds that same night:

> "Roundup good fellowship, service and cheer.
> Roundup the aims we hold so dear.
> Our hearts are filled with excitement, joy that resounds as we sing, sing out our Roundup round."

We travelled home again by train, but this time we went via Canada and Niagara Falls where we stopped at a classy hotel to enjoy a luncheon served on china plates! After a week of camping, eating in a fancy dining room wearing grubby clothes did seem strange – but it was glorious.

Roundup was during the summer between my sophomore and junior years of high school. Back home, our own troop continued planning the European trip for the next summer. Each of us had a pen pal, usually a Girl Guide, with whom we corresponded to make arrangements for our visit. Mine was named Jeanette who lived in Litchfield, England. Her family placed each of the girls in my troop into the homes of other members of Jeanette's troop while I stayed with Jeanette. Her uncle was the curator of the Litchfield Cathedral (the only English cathedral with three spires) and he gave us a tour of all the nooks and crannies of that church. In addition, Jeanette's family got us into the Joshua Wedgewood China Factory for a tour. The hospitality of the British in the Midlands of England was exquisite; tea and crumpets in bed every morning, rides around town with Jeanette's brother on his moped, and delicious food in spite of the poor reputation the Brits have about their cooking.

That summer we visited England, France, Belgium, Italy, Germany, Holland and Switzerland most often wearing our dress uniforms, saddle shoes, brown leather handbags and backpacks.

Adelboden, Switzerland is where the international home of all Girl Scouts and Girl Guides is located. It is high up, high on the mountain as is sung in the "Our Chalet" song:

"High up, high on the mountain, we founded Our Chalet.
High up, high on the mountain, we founded Our Chalet.
Its slopping roof and wide will shelter us without a care
And each and every Guide shall find a welcome there."

The ride up the mountain on a public bus was memorable for a couple of reasons. Looking out the window of the bus, all one could see was the bottom of cliffs below and very little of the road we were on. It didn't seem like there was room for error on the part of the driver. One slight mishap with the steering wheel on that steep and curving road and we'd all go off into the wild, blue yonder. The windows on the bus were not open, it was hot and the passengers hadn't been introduced to deodorant. I thought I'd suffocate. But one of the gals, having splashed Jean Nate on herself that morning, kept her nose in the crook of her arm all the way up the mountain.

At that time, Our Chalet had two buildings: the Main House and a separate structure called the Squirrel House. Only recently did I wonder why it was called that. Apparently, when it was first built, squirrels came to the window every morning. There were pecans in the shell left on the window sills and the squirrels would bang them together to crack them open. The noise they made was like an alarm clock telling everyone to 'rise and shine.' My assigned sleeping quarters were on the second floor of the Squirrel House where no cots – only mattresses were provided. I never saw or heard the squirrels while I was there. Perhaps they had decided to sleep in on those particular mornings.

One day we went down to a nearby town to swim in a municipal pool where the water was a very comfortable temperature. Looking up, while swimming, we could see snow on the tops of the mountains surrounding us. Perhaps that would not be an unusual sight for avid skiers, but for this city girl, the contrasting view was extraordinary.

The meals served at Our Chalet at that time consisted of cheese, breads, vegetables and fruit—no meat except on Sunday. Few animals were adept at grazing in the mountain terrain except for goats. So goat cheese was part of most meals. Besides meat on a Sunday, a serving of some special jam/jelly was on the tables at breakfast time. Unfortunately, I can't remember what that jam was except that I couldn't spread it on my toast thick enough; it was so good.

Italy presented some unusual problems that we were not accustomed to dealing with. The Italian boys liked to pinch our butts; so none of us wanted to be at the back of the pack and available for acts of affection. As a result, when walking in a group each of us would keep trying to get in front and be stumbling over each other. At a beach on the Indian Ocean, there was a ladder that allowed you slide down and into the water. At the bottom were the boys who would call out, "Hey Baby," and wait for us to come down so they could pinch our bums.

We tried to negotiate a ride through the Grand Canal on gondolas. In spite of no fluency in Italian, we thought we had successfully arranged a good deal for a romantic tour on a "barco." Unfortunately, the gondoliers took our money but steered the gondolas through the back passages where we saw people throwing their garbage out their windows into the canal. It was hardly romantic and the gondoliers didn't even sing "Volare."

My parents had limited funds to give us to buy souvenirs. Harriett suggested that I buy one thing from each country that might always remind me of this trip abroad. I bought a symbolic bracelet charm in each country, city, town, or cathedral we visited, including one from the World's Fair, which was held in Brussels, Belgium that year. At home, I had a total of twenty-five interesting charms to put on a sterling silver bracelet. (See Girl Scout memorabilia in Appendix A.)

After traipsing through Europe for approximately six weeks, we returned to Zeebrugge, Belgium to reboard the ship heading back to New Jersey and home. Our dresses and sport clothes had been stored on the ship while we wore our uniforms on the continent. It was a treat to get out of those uniforms and wear our casual clothes on the ship. (We put on fancy clothes to wear to the Captain's Dinner while we were out at sea and were allowed to drink champagne on that occasion.) Our accommodations on board were the least expensive available; somewhere near the very bottom of the ship with no windows and therefore no view of the ocean. These staterooms were tiny, crowded and offered two sets of bunk beds per room. The ship went through a bad storm on the voyage home and everyone was sick. The tendency when feeling nauseous was to run for your room. We had to be reminded to "throw up over the side." An announcement came over the intercom several times reminding everyone to keep their fingers away from the door jams because all those heavy doors kept slamming. Arriving in New Jersey, it was common to see lots of passengers wearing broken eyeglasses.

During the summer in between high school and college I worked as an assistant counselor of a bike unit at a Girl Scout camp. Our campers were the oldest and our unit was the furthest from the main camp. One of the camper's parents owned a pizza parlor and they came to the back gate many evenings to drop off pizzas for the counselors. We had friends come around when the campers were supposed to be asleep to enjoy the pizzas in the unit camp house. Other visitors included a pair of skunks. Because of their stripes, we knew them as "Flower" and "Yardley." They would enter the front of our tent one by one, clumsily bumping into the trunks under our cots sniffing for food and go out the back flap of the tent. We never made a sound and they continued on their way without ever spraying us. Even so, they smelled something awful. How do they mate with such a stink? My role in the bike unit that summer was to ride at the back of the pack to be the sweeper (to herd in stragglers) and make minor bike repairs such as broken bike chains. The view from that vantage point was quite amusing: all those fannies going back and forth and up and down on narrow wheels. The main camp would send ahead our tents, food, and sleeping bags to our destinations. The members of the bike unit would peddle about twenty miles per day to our scheduled camp site. Once there we would set up the tents, gather firewood, make a campfire to cook our supper and after charring our S'mores[8] for dessert, sing some Girl Scout songs tell ghost stories and collapse in our sleeping bags to enjoy a very sound sleep. The next morning we had cereal, packed sandwiches, peddled off to the next destination and repeated the whole camping process. One trip required us to visit a Girl Scout camp on an island where we camped for several days. We peddled our bikes onto a ferry to get there and back. It was a summer full of adventure and exercise, which left little time to think or get nervous about my starting college that fall. At the end of summer, the camp director arranged for the counselors to have lobster. She stood at the front of the mess hall and showed us step-by step how to crack open and eat lobster

---

8 A camping favorite of graham crackers with melted marshmallows and chocolate prepared over an open flame.

including the tomalley[9]. I now could eat lobster seven days a week, if I could afford it.

Often, when I fix something or make something out of nothing to solve a problem, I am asked, "How did you know how to do that." My answer is simply this, "I was a Girl Scout."

---

9   The green substance in the belly of the lobster that serves as a liver and pancreas. It is considered a delicacy.

CHAPTER 5

A Nurse Becoming

How in the world did I end up enrolling in nursing school? I was never a candy striper. My one experience in a hospital was via the Girl Scouts. Our troop was working on some kind of service badge. Mrs. Ray, our leader made arrangements for us to go to the city's general hospital one afternoon a week to help out wherever needed. This general hospital is where the indigent patients of the city were admitted. It was less than luxurious. It's strange that I can't remember one thing about my own experience, but I do recall my sister Pam's vividly. She liked to mess with and style peoples' hair. On our first day in one of the women's wards she ended up combing out and giving one of the patients a hairdo. This lady was very old, very wrinkled, had no teeth and drooled a lot. When my sister finished the task, the patient reached up, grabbed my sister by the neck and kissed her all over her face. After wiping the drool off herself and having a heart attack, Pam vowed never to touch another patient ever again. Each week she reported to the hospital, signed in, walked straight down the center corridor and out the back door. She sat on the back steps until it was time to go. She did put in her time and got a badge just like the rest of us.

My desire to go into a nursing program was likely stimulated in two ways: During the sophomore or junior year in high school, our Girl Scout leader (the same Mrs. Ray) thought it would be a good idea to investigate college/career choices. To kill two birds with one stone, she made arrangements for us to visit a state teachers college that also offered a collegiate nursing program. This way we could learn about careers and educational options in teaching as well as nursing.

As we entered the front door of the hospital to meet Miss Dillon, the director of nursing, there was an elderly man waiting for a family member to pick him up as he was being discharged. With him was a student nurse. The patient was thanking that student profusely. "You took such wonderful care of me. When you came into the room I knew I would be OK." I thought to myself, "Wow, what a wonderful feeling it must be inside to receive that kind of genuine praise. I'd like to be in a position to offer special skills and be that valuable and helpful to others."

Another compelling reason for considering nursing school was that I was scared silly about sickness and death. There was a girl younger than I that went to our church. Overhearing adults talk about how she had a headache one day and was dead the next made me crazy with worry. Where I had occasional migraine headaches, surely death would strike me down very soon. The evening prayer we recited each night did nothing to soothe my fears:

> "Now I lay me down to sleep
> I pray the Lord my soul to keep.
> If I should die before I wake
> I pray the Lord my soul to take."

I did not want to die before morning and I didn't want the Lord or anyone else to take my soul away while I was sleeping.

One of the girls in my scout troop had an episode of vomiting. She was admitted to the hospital for an emergency appendectomy. She reported to us that if she hadn't had the operation in time, she would have died. I worried about all these stories so much. How would I know if I or a member of my family was really sick? What would I do? How could I help? "Become a nurse and understand about the body and sickness. That was the answer," I reasoned.

The day I announced to my mother that I decided to become a nurse was dreadful. She ranted and raved. "I expected you to be a teacher. I don't want a daughter of mine cleaning up other peoples' dirty bodies. No you can't. I won't let you." Eventually I was able to get a word in edge-wise to explain that I planned to enroll in a five-year baccalaureate nursing program, would graduate with a bachelor's degree and with a couple more science courses could even teach science in elementary school. In addition, I would be eligible to sit to take the state licensing exam and become a Registered Nurse. Many, many years later, my mother confessed that that was one time she had been wrong.

My grandmother gave me a pair of white shoes and hose as a graduation from high school gift. It would be light years before I would wear them and actually walk into a patient's room to initiate patient contact. The first year and a half (3 semesters) consisted of course work on the college campus. We studied chemistry, physics, math, philosophy, English, art, music, anatomy and physiology and even physical education. The summer in between we took courses in microbiology, pharmacology and the history of nursing up on the hill at the school of nursing.

Nine of us lived on the college campus our freshman year because there weren't enough rooms at the nurses' residence. What we came to realize was that eight of the nine of us were Protestants. It turns out that Miss Dillon, The Director of Nursing, was a convert from being a Protestant to becoming a Catholic. The one Catholic in our group admitted at the time of her interview with Miss Dillon that she hadn't gone to church that Sunday morning. That fact doomed her to living with us Protestants on the college campus. What a favor Miss Dillon bestowed on us. We had a ball living in the real campus environment and we were therefore in the thick of the hazing of freshmen on campus. I twirled the hula hoop around my hips by the hour in front of the administration building. Nursing students were told to wear white gloves. The upperclassmen would flick their cigarette ashes on our gloves and then scold us for wearing dirty gloves. "What kind of a nurse are you? Clean up your act." At night we'd be awakened and ordered to go down to the dorm living room to sing. I thought all of the antics were pretty funny and unfortunately giggled a lot. So I was singled out quite often to sing solos. Where I flunked glee club in junior high school, my audience laughed uproariously through all my off-key renditions. From then on through graduation five years later I was known as "Gigs."

We managed to cause our share of trouble living in the campus dorm also: toilet paper fights, putting saran wrap over the toilets and then putting the seat down and throwing cold water over the shower stall when someone was taking a shower. One Friday night I had a date to go to the YMCA for a community swim. I had my bathing suit and towels in a train case (a small square suitcase). My date lifted me off my feet and carried me down the dormitory walk. Someone called to me from the window and I shouted back, "Hey, we're eloping!" Then I hear, "This is Mrs. Campbell (the housemother) you put her down." On Monday morning I was summoned to the Dean of Women's office. My offence: *man handling on campus.* My punishment: *roomed for one week.* (I was allowed to come out of my room for classes and meals.) My date, a senior guy, was called into the chambers of the Dean of Men. He was admonished, "Don't do your *funny business* on campus. Go elsewhere." (He was not roomed or punished in any way.)

Three of my Protestant classmates had dates to go to the movies with some guys from a near-by army base. It was a weeknight when general dating was not allowed. So they signed out

"Newman Club." Unfortunately, Lorrie left her purse in the theater. The manager called the college the next day to report the lost purse. Lorrie and her two buddies were *bagged* and suspended from school for one week. Imagine the nerve – signing out for a meeting of the Catholic Newman Club when they weren't even Catholic!

It wasn't all fun and games by a long shot. There was a lot of pressure on me to maintain a minimum of a B average. That was required to stay in the nursing program and to continue receiving the scholarships awarded to me at high school graduation. Two semesters of World History were almost overwhelming: so many countries changing their names and boundaries every two minutes, so many cultures, so many people – there's no beginning and hopefully no end to all that stuff. College Math was confusing. That was where we were introduced to working with numbers in a different base other than base ten. They called it modern math.

In the second semester sophomore year we began Medical/ Surgical Nursing, familiarly known to nursing students as Med/ Surg. *Nursing Process*, we learned was a system of thinking upon which nursing interventions are based. It requires subjective and objective assessments. Objective assessments are data that are measureable like temperature, blood pressure, laboratory results, etc. Subjective assessments are those that require interpretation of a patient's statements and behaviors.

Finally, I got to put on my white shoes and hose to meet a patient and do a subjective assessment. Because we were not in the hospital to do any hands on patient care, we had to wear our ugly, brown lab coats. So here it goes for me! Converse with your assigned patient and then write up a process recording like: he said, I took this to mean, so I said, and then he said and so on. Right off the bat confusion reigned.

"Hello, I'm Miss daMaglia. How are you today?"

"I didn't know it was raining out. When did it start?"

"No, it's not raining out."

"Well, why are you wearing a raincoat?"

"This isn't a raincoat, it's my lab coat."

"Oh, no, you're from the lab? (Very angry) I don't want any more blood tests. I'm black and blue from all those needles. Come back another time but not today. Please leave me alone. Go away."

"I'm sorry I upset you. I didn't come to do any tests. I just wanted to visit with you for a few minutes."

"I'm tired, Miss. I just want to be left alone to rest."

My very first patient threw me out!!! How I wrote this all up following the approved process recording format I can't remember. I probably fudged it to look/sound like something significant had occurred. I know now that the proper way to initiate conversation with a patient is to say who you are and what you do. Happy I was to learn that future patient contacts would not require wearing a lab coat (or a raincoat). As for those shoes from my grandmother and subsequent pairs – they were too short and no doubt account for why I have bunions and hammertoes today.

Nursing education has two components: theory and clinical practice. The theoretical part teaches diseases by body system and with each disease the symptoms, etiology, prevention, treatments and nursing considerations. For example; the unit on the reproductive system includes the topic of breast cancer and the importance of Breast Self Examination as a method of early detection. So often nursing students identify with some of the diseases and symptoms and think they might have whatever was being described. After the presentation on breast cancer, the instructor said, "I will now give you an extra 15 minutes at break time so you can go to your rooms and do your own breast self exams." The first place I put my hand, I felt a lump. "It has to be all in my head," I thought.

However, after class I headed over to the student health office because the "lump" was still there! Motherly Mrs. Mullins had me undress in one of the examining rooms while she called Dr Jacques. He was on call for students that month. Through the curtain I heard her side of the conversation: "I have a young student nurse here who has just been studying about breast tumors and thinks she feels a lump. Yes, I know (little giggle)." I was feeling foolish.

Dr Jacques arrived, checked out my lump and then instructed Mrs. Mullen, "Get one of Giulia's parents on the phone with two witnesses on this end so we can obtain permission for surgery and general anesthesia." I asked Dr. Jacques why I couldn't have spinal anesthesia rather than general. With a mischievous grin he replied. "Sure, we could give you a spinal from the neck down and then you'd stop breathing." (Reminds me of what happened to my poor frog in the nursing lab which is explained on page 58.)

That afternoon I was admitted to the surgical unit I had been assigned to for my own clinical experience that week. Some of my own patients came by to wish me well. I was okay with this dilemma for while. I figured I would use this experience to support other women who were having the same experience. Then I saw my name on the surgical schedule for the next day: "Giulia daMaglia, breast biopsy, question of radical mastectomy." I was still handling it all pretty well until two unprofessional staff members came in to prep me for surgery. They shaved my entire chest in case it would become a mastectomy and they chatted with each other, oblivious of me and my plight. That's when some little tears formed and dripped out of the corners of my eyes. These two chicks didn't notice that I was starting to fall apart.

Fortunately, Miss B. came to see me. She's the instructor who had been teaching about breast cancer that morning. "It's a good thing I had your class or I wouldn't have known about this tumor." She gently replied, "It would have made itself known to you eventually. Remember that you will be NPO (nothing by mouth) after midnight, so I would advise you to take the barbiturate that has been prescribed for you this evening." Further, she asked, "Do you know how long it will take to fall asleep once the anesthesia is started?" I wasn't sure so she explained that I wouldn't even be able to count to 10.

I followed her advice, took the sedative and before I knew it, I was awakened and rolled down to the operating suite. Miss B. was wrong. I was asked to count backwards from 10 and never got to 8. Next, I found myself in the recovery room being taken care of by some of my classmates who were assigned to recovery that week. They were eager to tell me that I didn't have cancer. It was a benign fibro-adenoma. They also laughed at me because while I was semiconscious I had sat up suddenly, put my left hand over my right breast and recited the Pledge of Allegiance.

Most nursing students are not long out of high school. While other college students the same age can continue to be self-absorbed, nursing students dealing with patients in clinical assignments find themselves in the midst of other peoples' crises and they must put their beings aside and learn to provide comfort and apply/practice newly learned nursing skills. How did we do it? I believe we functioned by ignoring the whole picture of where we were personally, putting one foot in front of the other, concentrating on one task at a time and relying on our instructors to show us the way and protect us.

There's a real benefit to living in a nurses' residence once you start clinical experience. We all had single rooms because eventually nursing students would be working different shifts. More importantly, each floor of the nurses' residence had a large lounge. That was where everyone met for study breaks, snacks, knitting and smokes. (Honest, we really didn't yet connect the dangers of smoking with so many health risks.) It was where we all exchanged horror stories about what we'd gone through and seen. It's where we converted worry and concerns into laughter. One of my classmates was horrified when her patient handed her his glass eye and asked that she put it in his eye cup. He said he didn't know where he put the container. That sent us into gales of laughter as did the story of a man reaching for his urinal thinking it was apple juice. All these tales and making fun of them proved to be a catharsis that helped us deal with difficult situations.

We wore our nursing school caps with a sense of pride. After successfully passing the probationary period the school held a "capping ceremony" and placed the coveted caps on our heads. The cap was made of crinoline and shaped like an oval cupcake. Once you made it to the senior year, a narrow, black, velvet ribbon was attached around the bottom. At graduation, an inch-wide ribbon replaced the narrower one. Much as we loved our caps, there was one problem. They were not washable. During my pediatric experience I entered the room of my toddler patient. He had been very busy painting the sides of his crib with the contents of his diaper. What a mess! Where to start? I filled a plastic tub with water and was about to pick him up when he grabbed my cap with his "paint covered" hands. That was the end of my cap. Into the trash it went.

We had to spend one day during our pediatric rotation in the outpatient department. I was fascinated by a large glass jar on the shelf there. I t contained all the items that had been removed from various orifices of the pediatric patients. Young children love to put things in holes. In that regard the body provides several interesting locations in which to deposit small items: ears, noses and even vaginas and rectums. Extracted from these locations and displayed in that jar were things like buttons, marbles, checkers, peas, beans, uncooked macaroni, puzzle pieces (The state of North Carolina was there.) and bottle caps.

Josh was the name of one of my most special pediatric patients. He had a form of terminal cancer. Although he was about nine, he couldn't read or write because he had missed so much school due to his illness. He had a colostomy, which required cleansing via a small enema on most days. While we sat together in the bathroom waiting for the colostomy to drain, I would read Nancy Drew books to him. He loved those stories as much as I did. Josh didn't have much of an appetite and he didn't like what they served him for breakfast. Together we wrote a letter to the dietary department asking that Josh's favorite cereal (Fruit Loops) be sent up each morning. Fruit Loops arrived thereafter without fail. Sadly Josh passed away. A month later, Josh's mother came to the hospital to bring me a birthday cake. It was the day Josh would have had a birthday. We cried together.

Caps are rarely worn today. Considering the reason for wearing them in the first place, they don't make sense today. Originally, nurses wore caps to cover their hair. Early on, women rarely had the where-with-all to shampoo very often. Caps were intended to keep dirty hair from getting into wounds and sores. They surely were required by students at the Florence Nightingale School of Nursing in London. Now where many women wash their hair most every day, putting on a dirty cap seems illogical. Also, today, more and more men are entering the nursing profession. Can you picture a guy wearing a cap?

Our school uniforms were laundered in the hospital laundry. I think they used a pound of starch on each one. We put our blue uniforms and white aprons down the laundry chute each Friday. They were waiting for us in the basement of the nurses' residence each Sunday night. You had to force open the sleeves with both hands to get your arms into the opening. We learned how to sit without wrinkling the apron: bring each half of the apron back around to the front. Fold them over each other and then sit down. To pass inspection each day required that there be no hair on the collar, that one had bandage scissors, catheter clamp, pen, orangewood stick in the pocket and a black velvet bow at the neck. I shudder to think that we may have used one orangewood stick to clean the nails of more than one patient, but I don't remember having lots of them in my pocket.

Finally, for public health nursing we wore simple, blue, uniform, black shoes and carried a black bag. With no car, I was assigned to a section of the city area where I could walk from one client's home to another. With ill-fitting shoes, my feet took a beating and probably contributed further to my developing bunions. My supervisor added a different visitation to my assignment one day. She said the children in the family were behind on their immunizations. They lived on the second floor of a tenement but it was difficult for me to get up there because half of the stairs were missing. Inside the apartment I found that the existing furniture resembled the outside stairs – for example, just a frame of a couch with no cushions. But there was a working color TV that was broadcasting a baseball game that the father was watching. At home with the father was a little girl wearing the skirt of a dress as a diaper. There was a tub in the bathroom, which had fish in it. Someone gave the fish to the father, but they needed to be skinned and cleaned. He didn't know how to do it, so he left them in the tub until his wife got home to take care of the matter. I explained that I would be running an immunization clinic at the end of the week and expected that the little girl would be there to get her shots. He said he'd speak to his wife about it. I left wondering how I or anyone could make a dent in all the health and social problems of that one family. At night, I called the supervisor and asked, "What was all that about? Where I'm just a student, how did that family end up on my visitation sheet? What did you expect me to accomplish when my rotation here is so short?" "I just wanted you see how some people live." "Thanks a lot!"

Not too long ago one of my classmates who is now a neighbor said to me over pizzas, "The instructors really liked you a lot." That statement took me by surprise. I had no sense of that. In fact, I believed that I drove the instructors crazy with naïve questions about and approaches to problems. In a summer session we were studying the physiology of the heart and its response to various solutions. To do this we had to dissect a frog. (Don't read any further if you have a weak stomach.) First you have to paralyze the frog. To do this, you pin the frogs' legs on a board and then stick a "pithing" rod down its spine to wipe out the central nervous system. After I did this I asked the instructor if it was okay to unpin the frog's legs. "Giulia, did you think your frog was going to hop away somewhere with no spinal cord?"

Maybe my naiveté was refreshing – it seemed I was never in danger of being dismissed as incompetent. Also, I interpreted instructions very literally. Before taking care of a patient you had to know all about his/her condition, what meds and treatments were ordered. Then if you were to do a treatment for the first time, you read all about it in the Procedure Manual. You followed the instructions and steps in the Procedure Manual exactly. I did all of this in preparation for giving my first enema. After administering the enema, I ushered my patient to the bathroom to expel the liquid. I reminded him not to flush the toilet so I could observe the results. (That's what the manual said.) "Please ring the buzzer when you are finished." All went according to plan. Next I was to write up this treatment in the nurses' notes. But one must review what's going to be written with the instructor first. Unfortunately, I was not familiar with the appropriate wording for reporting the results of an enema: good, fair, excellent, etc. No. I stood in front of my instructor telling her the results, saying, "There were five pieces the size of a dime, about ten pieces the size of a quarter…." I couldn't go any further because she was sliding down the wall red in the face and laughing with tears streaming down her face. I stood stock still, erect and wondering what was so funny. She stopped me from writing "ten pieces of poop" in the nurses' notes.

There was one thing that worried me a lot during the beginning of my clinical rotations. I had never seen male genitals in the flesh. To my eyes, the pictures in Anatomy and Physiology textbooks did not present a pretty picture – nothing like the cute little packages the baby boys I babysat for had. I had no brothers and my father kept his private parts private. My mother had a made up name for that part of the male anatomy. She would say to my father, "Carl, keep your 'portabearances' covered." The sex education she provided was fraught with negatives. "All males will want is one thing. Don't let a man tell you you're protected from pregnancy because he's wearing a condom." "What's a condom?" I asked. My sister said there was one hanging on the music room door that afternoon. I said I thought it was a balloon. She said, "It was a condom blown up, you dummy."

I didn't have many dates in high school. My mother asked why I seemed to have only one-night stands. I didn't want to tell her that the dates I had wanted to get too chummy and that scared me off. So except for anatomical pictures, that was the state of my male knowledge at the beginning of my clinical nursing experience.

Still a probationer, I went to the hospital, as required, to check my patient assignment for the next day. I was due to take care of a young man (about my age) who was admitted with "vomiting for one week and fever of unknown origin." His vomiting meant I would have to take his temperature rectally. "Oh my God, what am I going to encounter when I take his temperature? How is he going to feel about a young student nurse getting that close to his portabearances?"

I hardly slept that night with worry. The next morning I ate my breakfast in the hospital cafeteria and then headed to the unit I was assigned to. On my way to the nurses' station I detoured into the little conference room, threw up in the waste basket and then continued on my way. Taking a very deep breath, I went into my patient's room and introduced myself, "Good morning. I'm Miss Vitals and I'm here to take your Maglia." He didn't notice my faux pas. He was so sick an elephant could have entered the room and he wouldn't have cared. So I proceeded to take his temperature. Much to my surprise, when I raised his buttocks to insert the thermometer, there was nothing to see! The portabearances were in the front and out of view. I don't know when or where I finally did see male genitalia, but after that worrisome experience, I didn't really care anymore. I had wasted too much mental energy on that subject.

Life as a nursing student went on. I learned a lot, worried about doing everything just right and enjoyed being a patient advocate. I grew personally and professionally. When it came time to do our stint of night duty, I was assigned to the intensive care unit where it is daytime 24/7. One of my classmates, TMM, pulled night duty on the surgical ward. She had it easy because many of the patients there slept at night. So TMM called me to say, "This is the emergency room. Prepare for the admission of a severely burned patient." I hustled to get a bed ready. Then she called to say, "The patient was DOA." (Dead on arrival.) The next time she called, I caught on.

I did pay her back. On our surgical rotation we served as scrub nurses in the morning handling the instruments and holding incisions open with retractors. In the afternoons we prepared surgical packs for the next day's scheduled operations. We taped the packs closed with a special tape that would produce stripes if the package survived the rigors of the autoclaving process; I marked TMM on any of my packages that looked like they would fall apart. TMM would get reprimanded for unsatisfactory bundling.

A leadership role in any group or organization has always attracted my interest and enthusiasm. This continued to be the case as I pursued my studies in the nursing program. I held various positions in our school's student government, but what was most exciting was that during our second year, I formed a nurses' basketball team to compete against the sororities down on the campus. Granted some of my classmates had no idea how to dribble the ball or even what basket to shoot at. If the ball came their way, they panicked and ran away from it. Those gals became our cheerleading squad. The rest of us athletic types made up the team of players. Four nights a week the whole class met in the gym of the nurses' residence. The cheerleaders were in one corner practicing their routines and the rest of us were on the court working up some useful and even some "tricky" moves. When we registered for the basketball tournament, the athletic director was first shocked and then amused. There had never been a basketball team of nurses before.

We arrived (cheerleaders and basketball players alike) packed into three cars cheering and making a hell of a racket all along the route from the nurses' residence to the gym on the college campus. We beat the first sorority as if they were standing still. The next game was more of a challenge, but we were never behind. Finally we were scheduled to play the third sorority whose members included a bunch of jocks. We got off to a slow start, but the cheering was so loud and intense that we couldn't help but respond and of course came out on top. For all that we won silver basketball bracelet charms at the athletic banquet at the end of the year. Nursing students had never competed in athletics before, so it was an interesting phenomenon that we should all be there to collect our silver basketballs.

We had one classmate who could not and would not swim. There was a degree requirement that every graduate had to demonstrate the ability to swim one length of the pool. Many of us tried to teach Mavis to swim without success. Three of us entered a pact with her. I would swim the length of the pool under her and two other classmates would swim on either side of her. It worked! She met the requirement! The physical education professor ignored the support that was given, but said to me, "So you swam one length underwater; let's see if you can do 120 feet underwater." (That's two lengths of the pool.) I took a deep breath and started at the shallow end, swam to the deep end, turned around and went back to the shallow end all without coming up for air. I thought I'd die, but I made myself do it and the professor was holding out her hand to help me out of the pool at the end. At the same banquet where we received the basketball charms, I was given a silver fin bracelet charm marked "120 feet underwater."

During the junior year I was our school's representative to the state's student nurses' association and then was elected president of the state organization. In that role I then became a member of the board of the national student nurses' association. All of the meetings I attended at the state, regional and national levels caused me to miss some class time. However, I had an incredible advisor. She coached me about my leadership duties, Robert's Rules of Order, class work I was missing, and life. She drove me to the airport when I needed to travel. She became the person and nurse I most wanted to be like when I graduated.

There was one state meeting when my personal advisor could not accompany me. Another faculty member took her place. After the session when we returned to her car, we discovered a flat tire. She called her travel insurance plan. A mechanic arrived an hour later to put on the spare tire. About fifty miles later we had another flat tire and no spare. Again she called for assistance and was advised that it would be another hour before anyone could come to us. She said she really needed to use a bathroom. We were parked on the side of the road outside a fenced-in section of a hospital. We walked around the perimeter of the fence until we came to what was the dormitory for medical residents. First we went down a short flight of stairs and opened a door of a janitor's closet. I suggested she "pee in the bucket." But she refused. Then we headed back up the stairs to where a medical student was manning the reception desk. Unfortunately, my instructor's bladder didn't hold on with those last few stairs. That's when I heard her shoes squishing with each step. We were directed to a rest room around the corner. There she emptied out her shoes, removed her underpants and panty hose, wrung them out and wrapped them in paper towels and attempted to pull herself together. We were laughing hysterically and I almost wet my own pants. Then suddenly she turned serious, "Don't you ever breathe a word of this to anyone." I never told a soul and when we met up in various situations I managed to look at her and block out the vision of her shoes filled with urine.

Every spring the state's student nurses would meet at a large auditorium in the center of the state to celebrate Florence Nightingale Day. About two thousand students arrived on buses dressed in the uniforms of their school. They entered the light-dimmed auditorium through different doors carrying lighted candles. As president, I was on the stage to witness this sight – a beautiful and inspirational sight I shall never forget. Here were all my student nurse sisters. We share so much, we have been through a lot. I had goose bumps from head to toe.

I don't remember much about the program or who the key note speaker was. I was probably worrying about the little speech I had to give. A faculty member from my school had spent time with me practicing the diction, pacing and overall delivery of it. What I kept stumbling over was the pronunciation of Florence Nightingale. I kept saying Florence "Night-In-Gale" when it was supposed to be "Nighting-gale."

My college and nursing school years ended on a high. At graduation I received the "Student Nurse of the Year Award" presented by my classmates, the Alumnae Award presented by the faculty and the Margo Boyd Award presented by the district's state nurses association. The latter was a cash award, which paid for my first pair of contact lenses.

Through it all, I did suffer a loss – 35 pounds!

CHAPTER 6

Careers:
How Many Hats *Is* One Allowed to Wear?

Chances are most everyone could write a book about their jobs or careers – especially my father. No one loved his job more than he. He drove a bus pretty much on the same route for over 50 years. His enjoyment of driving and his entertainment of the passengers is detailed in Chapter 2.

From about age 12 to 16 I babysat several nights a week as well as on Saturdays. On my sixteenth birthday, on a windy and rainy day, I walked to Kresge's Five and Dime to fill out a job application. I expected to simply complete the paperwork and then wait for a phone call. Instead, soaking wet and looking like a drowned rat, I was interviewed by the store manager and then taken upstairs to an office area where I was taught how to work a cash register and the correct way to count out the change to a customer. I was to start work on the toy counter the very next Friday from five to nine and the next day from nine to five. My salary would be sixty-five cents per hour. The toy counter might seem like an enjoyable spot in a five and dime, but it wasn't. Little kids and sometimes adults would try to steal stuff. I did my best to keep an eagle eye on the people and on the merchandise. But it stressed me out.

As Easter and springtime rolled around, my job was to wind up all the metal mechanical bunnies and rabbits so they could all hop along the counter. I recall that they were twenty-nine cents and all that winding left my fingers raw. Then as summer approached, I was expected to stand on the sidewalk in front of the store and demonstrate the hula hoop. By the hour I would twirl my hips to keep the hula hoop in motion. The sailors from a nearby naval base appreciated my talent but they never bought any hoops. Interestingly however, many of those sailors went to the dry good counter and emptied out the entire supply of yarns. Lots of sailors knit while on long term sea assignments.

I continued to work at Kresge's every Friday night and Saturday through my high school years. One Friday night a cat went up a pole somewhere in the city and caused a transformer to blow. Most of the city lost power. We high school girls at the back of the store and in total darkness were squealing, giggling, calling out to each other, and groping around. Quite honestly, we were enjoying this sudden and unusual event. I'm not sure how long the power outage lasted, but when the lights did come back on, almost everything was missing from the counters, including my own. How shocking it was to me that while the salesclerks couldn't even see each other, customers were stealing the goods right from under us.

Because my five-year college program included summer sessions, I was not able to seek employment again until after my college/nursing graduation, which occurred in early December. I had plans to marry in mid December. Therefore, I had sent a letter to a hospital near where I would be living inquiring about employment options. The answer I received stated that I would be considered for working rotating shifts and every other weekend. In the meantime, my mother had had a call from the director of nurses in my home town wanting to offer me a teaching job at her hospital. I met with her and, as a newly married woman; she presented an offer that was too good to pass up: days only, week-ends and several weeks off in the summer and a salary of $87.50 per week. I signed a contract, but I wasn't happy with that job. For one thing I was under the supervision of a disorganized senior faculty member who treated me as if I were her puppy dog and a "gofer." But she suffered from an attack of appendicitis, was oper-ated on and out of commission for six weeks.

Suddenly, "wet behind the ears" it was up to me to step up to the plate to coordinate the clinical experiences of students both in pediatrics and obstetrics. The pediatric nursing staff was understanding, cooperative and helpful. The obstetrical nurs-ing supervisor, on the other hand, went out of her way to insult me and embarrass me in front of doctors and staff whenever she could. I may have been over my head with responsibility, but I made sure the students' clinical learning experiences were not negatively affected.

After recuperating from her appendectomy, my teaching supervisor returned and she resorted back to treating me as her personal attendant. "Where's my pencil?" "Where did I leave my cigarettes?" "Put these grades in the rank book." "What time is it?" I had grown so much during her six-week absence and now I was back to feeling like a useless nobody.

I was all ears at around that time to hear there was an open-ing at a state hospital for an instructor for Licensed Practical Nurse students. It involved bringing students from three affili-ated LPN programs to the state hospital to learn about caring for children and adolescents with long-term illnesses. It would be my responsibility to develop an approved curriculum and provide the clinical experiences for the affiliating students. That hospital, its patients, the nursing staff and my curriculum design was a winning combination for me. I was happy, I felt productive and I was appreciate and respected. Other schools became interested in the program being offered and petitioned to send their students to us, also. By then, I was expecting my first baby and two very qualified people with advanced degrees were hired to replace me. Prior to my going on maternity leave, a new speech therapist was hired and was given an office next to mine. His name was Ed Kodak. I invited him to accompany me to coffee a break in the cafeteria so I could introduce him to some of the nurses on the staff. "Please meet Mr. Polaroid," I said. That became his name for as long as he worked there. When he learned I had had a baby boy, he sent me flowers and a note saying, "I'm sorry your violet has a stem."

Before leaving full-time employment, I decided to run for the Board of Health in our small rural town. It bothered me that there were no visiting nurse services available to our residents. Should a patient from our town be ready for discharge from a hospital, but need some nursing care, that person would have to go to a nursing home instead, because nursing services did not exist for them. I judged this situation to be unfair and unnecessarily expensive. My assessment of the situation fell on the deaf ears of the selectmen and community leaders. I determined that a little political clout was necessary to change matters.

Winning the election was comparatively easy next to all the problems that the members of the Board of Health had to deal with. The pleasant news was that I was able to successfully write a joint federal grant with the director of a Visiting Nurse Association in a nearby city for funds to initiate and support home visits by Registered Nurses and well baby clinics. The other responsibilities of a Board of Health in a small town were far from glamorous. The board members were unsalaried but received remuneration for some of the tasks they performed.

There were inspections of new sewerage installations, mostly septic tanks and leeching fields. The town, of course, didn't have public sewerage treatment facilities and still doesn't. So I would take my measuring tools, put my baby in the car seat and go off to meet a contractor to inspect his sewerage disposal construction. Seeing me drive up, he would ask, "Can I help you?" "I'm from the Board of Health to inspect your work before you can close."

I ignored the incredulous "YOU?" and went about my business of measuring size, depth, slope, etc.

Restaurant inspections had to done regularly *and* unannounced. There were several restaurants in town, but only one was of concern. It was like a truck stop and the owner had trouble keeping up with the simplest of mandated codes. We gave the owner lots of warnings, both verbally and in writing: "Thelma, you have to keep this food in the refrigerator." "The food has to be covered." "You must wear a hairnet over your long hair or keep it tied up." "You must keep your dog out of the kitchen and out of the restaurant for that matter." She acted so appreciative of our suggestions and our patience even giving me a package of Life Savers once. I opened it in the car and saw that it had to have been 100 years old – all soft and crumbly and unpalatable. Poor Thelma couldn't even keep her Life Savers edible. We closed her down temporarily several times, but finally had to close her restaurant permanently.

Then there were the beach inspections. That small town had twelve public beaches and one private beach associated with a boys' camp. Each week during the summer months I would visit each beach (again with baby in tow), to take water samples. Each bottle was suspended from a wire hook. I would walk into the water up to my hips, dip the bottle in, cap it and drive all thirteen bottles to a state laboratory for testing. The only samples that regularly had high levels of E-coli were from the boys' camp. Swimming would have to be cancelled for a week until the next improved sample came back.

Maintaining the town dump was a nuisance. Pickers would set the dump on fire so they could retrieve the remaining scrap metal and carry it away. But the fumes and smoke from the burning was unacceptable to nearby residents and a fire hazard in general. The volunteer fire department members, the police and the three of us on the health board took turns chasing would-be pickers away. With the recycling and land fill programs in operation today, pickers must have had to seek other forms of recreation or employment.

Being on the board of health was a thankless job. You hear nothing but complaints. "There are too many mosquitoes around my yard this year." "Well we did aerial spraying yesterday, but we can't prevent the mosquitoes coming here from other towns." "My next door neighbor bought a horse and it comes up to the side of my house where my daughter's bedroom is and urinates outside her window. It stinks and now we have flies all over the place." "Ok we'll check it out and have the owner put up a fence further away from your house." "The garbage man dripped watery garbage on my driveway this morning." I took care of all these complaints as best I could – but it was most annoying.

One complaint came from a mother whose son had captured and was playing with a field mouse who finally bit the boy. Her husband was associated with the military, so the mother called the physician on the base to ask what to do. She was advised that the mouse had to be examined for rabies to determine if her son would need shots to prevent rabies. She needed to call the board of health. The mother didn't tell the doctor that she had beaten the mouse to smithereens. She called me and again did not tell me the condition of the mouse either. I contacted the animal control officer, the postmaster and the town druggist. The mouse could not be sent to the state laboratory in the mail because it was a warm blooded animal. (Only snakes can be sent via the post office.) But the post master provided a suitable mailing box. The druggist put some dry ice in the box and the animal control officer with protective gloves packed the mouse in the box on the dry ice. I learned later that the animal control officer drove a school bus and didn't have a car that day. He couldn't drive the bus all the way to the state's laboratory; so he drove to a railroad station and shipped it from there. The mouse had a ride on a school bus and a train before finally arriving at the lab for examination. The report came back to the board: "Mouse head of town X too deteriorated to examine." Had they looked a little more closely, they would have seen that the mouse had a big smile on his face. After all, how many other mice get to leave this world with such adventure? In mouse society he would have been considered a world-wide traveler.

Farmer Hardy had a vegetable garden and stand on the corner of one intersection in the town. On the opposite corner was a quirky guy, named Amos, who opened up an antique shop in a rundown shack. He apparently lived in the back with his dog. One day Farmer Hardy's son was teasing the dog, so the dog bit him. Hardy had a temper and he shot the dog with bird shot. It wasn't enough to kill the dog, but the dog was miserable and in pain. So Amos called the police to come and shoot him and get him out of his misery. The police didn't know the dog had bit anyone, so they shot the dog and Amos dug a **shallow** grave in his backyard to bury the dog. Later in the day, not knowing her husband's treatment of the dog and its demise, Mrs. Hardy decided to take her son to the doctor. The wound was cleaned up and the doctor instructed her to call the Board of Health to have the dog quarantined ten days to be sure it didn't have rabies. By the time I was alerted to this dog bite incident another day had gone by.

All these events occurred on a hot, hot Memorial Day weekend. I sent the animal control officer to Amos' shack to collect the dog and have him placed in quarantine. Amos instead pointed to where the dog was buried. The animal control officer attempted to exhume the dog so his head could be sent for testing. As it had been very hot and the grave very shallow, the remains were disgusting. Our animal control officer vomited up both his breakfast and his lunch. Mr. Hardy's son therefore had to have his shots. That's what you get when you take matters into your own hands and shoot a dog with bird shot.

The town finally had visiting nurse services, but four years of all those other crazy responsibilities was more than enough public service for me. I did get paid nine dollars per inspection and I used that money to buy additional pieces of my English bone china. However, I must admit that I learned some valuable lessons while on the Board of Health about how to get things done. They proved to be very helpful to me in future endeavors. For example, if you're trying to push through a program that you sincerely believe in but there are others who will likely oppose it, invite those people to serve on a committee to work with you. Listen to them attentively. Invite respected community members to speak for you on occasions such as town meetings. Give each of them typical questions that might be asked and provide the answers. That way it will appear that there is wide support for your plan.

Ultimately, I developed a set of operational strategies that became known later in my career(s) as Maglia's Methods. (They are itemized in Appendix A.)

If you must speak to a group trying to garner their support for what you are trying to do, start off by describing a problem that will pull at people's heart strings. Next, lay out the facts. Finally, end with a real and emotional short story. Don't entertain questions from the entire group. Instead end the presentation with a statement such as this, "I know you are all pressed for time, so if anyone has questions, please feel free to see me at the back of the room when the meeting is over." This way you prevent people in the audience from hearing any negative ideas they hadn't considered themselves.

It was when I announced that I would not run for reelection that I began to receive phone calls that were not complaints. Bebe, the town's very bright newspaper correspondent called to compliment me on all that I had accomplished and begged me to reconsider my decision. "Thanks for the positive strokes," I said. "But too much more of this stuff might lead me to get a gun myself – and it won't be loaded with bird shot."

At one point during my tenure on the Board of Health, a friend wrote into the TV program *What's My Line?*, suggesting I be an invited guest with my line being a "town sewer inspector." I received a telegram from the casting director asking if I could be available for taping in the fall. "That's when we do our recording for the next year's programs," she explained. My hairdresser said he would go to New York with me to tend to my hair styling needs. I made a pale green lacy dress to have ready for my debut. My thought was that I should be all dolled up looking like anything but a sewer inspector.

What's My Line? was a guessing game in which panelists attempted to determine the occupation of the contestant. The host of the show was John Charles Daly and the regular panelists wearing blindfolds were Dorothy Kilgallen, Bennett Cerf and Arlene Francis. The panelists were required to probe by asking only questions that would elicit either a "yes" or "no" answer. I believe the contestant received a prize if the panelists couldn't guess the "line." All summer I waited to hear from the casting director with instructions about when I was supposed to come to New York for taping. Finally, towards the end of summer, I called them. "Perhaps you've been trying to reach me while I've been away serving as a summer camp nurse. I've been wondering when you have me scheduled for taping." (I didn't want to sound too pushy.) "We're sorry. *What's My Line?* is going off the air and we'll only be showing reruns here on out."

All my thoughts of making the big time were dashed. I so envied Carol Burnett. How I'd have loved to have been discovered and given a role like she had – where I could clown around on stage, be silly, get out of control laughing and get paid big bucks. I'm much older now, but maybe I'll be discovered yet.

When my daughter was two, I decided it was time for me to return to school for a Masters Degree in Nursing. The timing was perfect because the government was awarding fellowships to nursing students in graduate programs with the stipulation that recipients continue working in the state where their education was offered for at least two years.

My selected course track included advanced clinical experiences, but focused as well on teaching and curriculum design. We were to learn how to incorporate new Audio/Visual techniques into our teaching strategies. The TV was not commonly used by teachers at that time. Our first assignment using the TV studio was for the students to pair up and together prepare a televised instructional clip, which would be shown to and be evaluated by other students. It didn't have to be related to nursing. Because it was Christmas time, I had the idea to do a demonstration of how to make a bow for a gift package. We pretended my partner was being hired for the holidays to do the gift wrapping in a department store and I was to teach her bow making. The camera was rolling, all was going according to plan except that I cut the center of the bow a little too far in. When the bow was tied to the package and then opened up, my student bow maker discovered that each petal came off in her hand. When she finished there was no bow – just a knot where the bow should have been. We kept smiling, acted as if everything was fine and kept a running dialog that concluded with, "You'll probably do better next time." When our production came over the closed circuit TV, our classmates were falling off their seats with laughter. So was the professor. The consensus was that our skit was a 100% success if comedy was our objective or our genre.

Next, we were to produce, individually, a ten-minute TV clip having something to do with our area of clinical nursing expertise. I can't remember what my topic was but I wore my white cap and uniform for taping. Unfortunately, TV recoding at that time did not reproduce white accurately. White became yellowish. So when I appeared on TV for my second presentation, I looked like I had egg yolk on my head and a dirty, yellowish looking garment on my body. The students' recollection of my previous comedy and now this gaudy showing had them roaring all over again. The professor's evaluation went something like this: "Giulia, your script and ideas are well-conceived. Perhaps you will need someone else to enact them because your presentations turn into comedy even when that's not what you intended."

In future teaching jobs I used TV quite often and successfully. In fact, at the end of my Masters Degree program I was required to do some practice teaching at a state university. There, given my background, I was asked to deliver a class on care of adolescents with long term illnesses. Gerry had been one of my patients at the state hospital where I had worked previously. He was born with an irreparable spina bifida and was wheel chair bound. Although mentally challenged, he was a pleasant, fairly independent and a very likeable guy. He said he'd like to come with me to my presentation and answer the students' questions about his life's experiences. The class was scheduled to be held in the university's TV studio with the whole class in attendance. The dean of the college of nursing was to attend also because she was to evaluate my teaching and report back to the graduate school where I was studying. Before starting class, I took Gerry to the book store and bought him a sweat shirt with the school's logo on it. He wore it for the taping. The students warmed up to Gerry who told about how he enjoyed boy scouts, who his friends were, his favorite meal (spaghetti and meatballs), etc. The class met the intended goal: That the students appreciate that having multiple handicaps does not mean life can't be pleasurable. The dean asked me to meet with her. She wanted to offer me a teaching position on her faculty. I was reluctant to accept at first because my daughter was by then only three. However, the dean explained it wasn't necessary for me to be on campus every day; I needed only to give the position my full time attention. For example it would be alright to prepare lectures and correct papers at home. I would, of course, have the responsibility to be in a hospital setting two full days a week to provide for the students' clinical learning and supervision. That September, I started as a full-time university professor.

ME - A PROFESSOR?

Am I now over my head joining a university faculty full of PhD's? Could I establish myself among faculty members who could argue cogently with the academic deans, whose vocabularies were rich, whose arguments were persuasive and philosophical and humorous and fascinating? I was in awe of these people who were now my colleagues.

Dutifully I went about the business of being a professor to baccalaureate nursing students usually in their junior or senior year of studies. Having had wonderful instructors during my own college years, I modeled my pedagogy after the style of my favorite ones.

Although my clinical expertise was in maternal and child health, my teaching assignment that first year included two rotations in a locked ward in a psychiatric hospital for chronically ill veterans. My students were a mature, lively and fun-loving bunch and together we muddled our way through the challenges of each psych rotation.

Most of the patients had been out of society for a very long time and were unaware of most things we take for granted. One strategy to address this limitation is called "reality therapy." We would bring a group of patients together and try to engage them in conversation about matters that were current or apropos the season. At one session my students introduced the subject of the spring flowers that were blooming at that time. They brought in roses, crocuses, daffodils and forsythia. They had hardly started the presentation when one patient took the rose and ate all the pedals. There he sat with the stem hanging out of his mouth. The staff called poison control and thankfully we learned that roses are not poisonous. The next week the students attempted a therapy session about current models of cars on the road and the cost of gas. They brought in miniature model cars. I sat next to the guy who ate the rose at the last presentation, and sure enough, he went to put the little Cadillac in his mouth. I grabbed it in time.

One student named Rob was to get a urine specimen from his incontinent patient for routine testing. He applied the condom collection unit correctly but the patient kept pulling it off. Rob followed him around until he wet his briefs. In the utility room he wrung out the pants into a specimen bottle and sent it to the lab. He cleaned the man up and put him in his usual Depends-type diaper. I had wondered what the students were all laughing about in the utility room. I laughed myself when I heard the story.

We brought the patients together to play softball, swim in the pool and picnic on the grounds. On the day of one of the patients' birthdays, the students brought in a cake and put six candles on top. (Of course, we didn't light them.) We started singing "Happy

Birthday" when one man grabbed some candles and put them in his mouth. Meanwhile 'birthday boy' put his fist in the middle of the cake and another guy suffered a seizure and fell on the corner of the table. He cut his forehead and required stitches. It was a hell of a party.

To be honest, it wasn't the most educational experience for the students. The goals they set for their patients were difficult to reach. Mostly we concerned ourselves with patient safety and activities that might make them happy and bring a smile to their faces. It seemed like we were babysitters. In following years, the college of nursing initiated contracts with acute psychiatric settings. With the drugs and treatments available today most mental illnesses can be managed without long term hospitalizations. In an acute setting one is likely to see improvements over a reasonable amount of time.

Being the new kid on the block may be the reason I was given five male students and only three females in my first clinical group for clinical practice in an obstetrical setting. I worried about how to arrange patient assignments during the obstetrical rotation for so many male students. Taking care of the babies in the nursery wouldn't be a problem, but would mothers in labor and delivery or on the postpartum unit object to having a male provide their nursing care? The evening before a clinical day I would approach a woman who would be an appropriate patient assignment for one of my students. This is the sales pitch I presented: "I am Professor daMaglia. I am a Registered Nurse and a professor of nursing at the university. I teach the nursing students who will be here tomorrow and the day after. We would appreciate the opportunity to provide the nursing care for you and Ms. Smith (the woman in the next bed) as well as your babies. My female students will be responsible for doing your physical care, so your privacy is honored. My male students are responsible for overseeing that you and your babies receive the best care possible. And I will be here offering my expertise to the students and you also." I don't recall any woman ever objecting. In fact, one new mother, at the end of the first day of care asked, "Could I have him for my nurse tomorrow?" Another woman in labor said to one of the male students, "I know you have to go to lunch, but could you leave your beard here? I need it for a focal point. [10] Please hurry back." That student drew a picture of his face with a beard and pinned it to the curtain in front of her.

It's not done today, but when I was doing clinical supervision in obstetrics, it was standard procedure to shave the public hair of a woman on her admission to labor and delivery. Shaving another person's skin is strange because you can't feel the razor's movement as when you shave yourself. To teach and explain the admission procedures, I would don a johnny, climb into a labor bed and issue instructions about what needed to be done. I even let the students take turns shaving me – NOT MY PUBIC HAIR OF COURSE – just my legs. They listened to my heart rate with the fetocope[11], opened and closed a sterile table, did all the appropriate charting, etc. I think I made it fun for them and helped them relax in this clinical environment where a patient's status can change quickly and sometimes seriously. The excitement of coaching soon to be parents, seeing their baby born and then caring for mother and baby afterwards was a thrilling experience. Most of the time all went well, but occasionally when complications arose; it was a heartbreaking situation for everyone. Usually the staff did not permit the students to be involved in that kind of emergency because they didn't have enough experience to know what to say or do.

Did I deliver any babies myself? Yes – three. It wasn't the plan, but it just happened that a baby couldn't wait and there I was.

I flunked a fair number of students. When my guts suggested that I would never want this student taking care of me or of someone I love, I would look for the reasons behind that feeling. One student, in particular, seemed to be careless about her

---

10   In this context, focal point refers to something for the woman in labor to look at (and study) during a contraction to provide distraction.

11   A fetoscope is a specially designed stethoscope placed on the pregnant woman's abdomen to listen for the fetal heartbeat.

responsibilities and professional behavior. During her first clinical experience in "Introduction to Professional Nursing" I found her in the women's ward with six chronically ill female patients. She was in the mirror over the sink combing her long blonde hair. As she primped, I heard her ask, "So ladies, what are we having for lunch today?" I never realized my arm could extend so far as I reached for her and pulled her out of the room. I watched her carefully after that and eventually had enough documentation to help her see that she was falling far short of meeting the objectives of the course and clinical expectations. My suggestion would be, "Perhaps it would be wise to drop out now and take a 'withdraw passing' grade rather than risk getting twelve credits of an F." She and many others would then thank me for my guidance and advice.

One of the first things I did when I came on the faculty was to start the College of Nursing's student organization. Students and I attended state conferences, sponsored poster presentations and enjoyed parties – including an evening cruise on a fishing boat.

At one point, I became chair of our college's curriculum committee. It became apparent to me that there must be a science to all this business of curriculum design. That thought prompted me to enroll in an evening class in a curriculum at a large university. In reviewing my work at the end of that one course, the professor suggested I consider matriculation[12] in the university's doctoral program. He said he'd be honored to be my advisor. It was my good fortune that the dean of my own college had funds to support doctoral studies for any of her faculty members who were matriculated and enrolled in doctoral studies. I was the only one who qualified for financial assistance and most all those monies were allocated to me. In addition, I had applied for and received a sabbatical leave for one semester. Everything came together perfectly for me. My graduate school advisor indicated that the writing and investigation I was doing for each of my doctoral course requirements suggested the topic for my doctoral thesis. He pointed out

---

12   To admit or be admitted into a group, especially a college or university.

that all my course work was adding substance and background to a potential doctoral research project.

My doctoral thesis investigated how students, prior to their entry into baccalaureate programs make decisions about selecting a school of nursing to attend. Getting the data, cataloguing it all and interpreting it was tedious, time consuming and exhausting. I wanted it all behind me as quickly as possible. The pressure and tension of the work caused me to lose twenty pounds. So many of my classmates remained ABD (all but dissertation), and I didn't want to be one of them. I passed my written comprehensive exams and finally the day came for my doctoral thesis defense. My advisor was present as was the associate dean of the college and other professorial judges. A nervous wreck, I recall nothing of what I was asked or what I answered. At last, I was asked to leave the room while my work was discussed. I paced the waiting area for about fifteen minutes. When I was invited back, the associate dean welcomed me with, "Congratulations Dr. daMaglia." There were a few more minor changes I needed to make before my thesis went out for printing, binding and then was catalogued in the library. I was invited to present my findings at a few research symposiums and hired to write recruitment brochures for several schools – but I was so tired of the whole subject, I didn't care whether I ever read my own thesis ever again.

So now I was Doctor daMaglia. I didn't feel one bit smarter than when I had started my doctoral studies. My new degree, to me, was an indication that I was one who could jump through hoops, one who was persistent and one who at least understood how demanding research really is.

Back at my own school, with my new degree in hand, the dean had plans for me. The nursing school was due for an accreditation visit by the National League for Nursing. The previous visit had awarded the school only a one year accreditation status and a one year provisional approval. I was given a leave of absence from my teaching duties and clinical obligations to attend to the coordination and writing of the next Self-Study Accreditation

Review. I tackled the project piece by piece and rode herd on the faculty to get their assignments written and often rewritten to my satisfaction. I spent a few days in New York City reading reviews by other schools who had received the full eight-year accreditation. Seven days a week I devoted to the challenge of getting an accurate report submitted that would garner our school a full accreditation.

After reviewing our Self Study Report, the NLN accreditors arrived to do a three-day reality check of our program. The first session was scheduled to be held in the provost's office. In attendance were the three accreditors, the dean, the provost and me. I sat next to the provost. The first statement made by the chief evaluator was, "Congratulations on such a well written and impressive report." Under the table the provost gave me a congratulatory nudge. The visit went extremely well and our college received a full eight year accreditation. The provost later held a wine and cheese reception for the school of nursing faculty to reward our success. He offered a toast that included "kudos to Dr. daMaglia and the dean for all their work."

During this time I also chaired an ad hoc university committee. The directive issued by the president was to gather data on all the honors that were awarded to students in all colleges/departments and possibly suggest a way to coordinate them into one large honors awards program. Our submitted proposal for a university-wide honors convocation was adopted by the president as was the suggestion that there be a university-wide honors program for qualified students. The provost began a search for a part-time honors director and the ad-hoc committee recommended me for the position. Given the recent accolades I had received from the National League for Nursing's accreditors, he offered me the position. Starting from scratch I wrote a curriculum that would allow all students of any major entering the university with a B+ or better academic performance in high school to enroll. Students who completed the honors requirements would then graduate as 'State Scholars.' While I developed this program, I continued teaching twelve contact hours of clinical nursing each semester.

Next, the provost announced he was looking for a faculty member to start a university advising program. Too many students entering the university as "undeclared" or on probation were dropping out. Many of my own nursing students used to bring their friends of other majors to me for advice. I loved the role of counseling, and the idea of providing academic advising on a university level really appealed to me. When I expressed my interest to the provost, he stated, "You'd be the perfect person for the position. You have done a great job getting an honors program off the ground. I can't let you drop it now, we'd risk losing it and that would be an unfortunate step backwards. If you really want to start the advising program, you'll have to give up your teaching obligations in the college of nursing." I agreed to do that. Now I was a mid-level university academic administrator with a special parking sticker for my car!

Was it difficult to essentially remove myself from the college of nursing faculty? No, not really. To be honest, I was looking for a change. Clinical instruction can be nerve wracking. I'm helping one student who's administering intravenous medications for the first time while I'm worrying what another student may be doing in another room. My students were placed in one of four areas each day: labor and delivery, newborn nursery, special care nursery and post-partum. To make matters more stressful, the labor and delivery and special care nursery units were on the third floor and the postpartum and regular nursery were on the second. Eight hours a day, two days a week I ran from one student/patient to another. If I had ten students and they each had one or two patients to care for, I was running around worrying about twenty or more people. From labor and delivery, "Please come and supervise me on using the fetuscope to check the baby's heart beat. I haven't done that before." Then from postpartum, "I have to give my patient an injection of RhoGam.[13] I've given injections before, but this med seems to be a bit complicated." I was ready for a change and a new challenge.

The advising program started with a make-shift advising room loaned to us by the career placement office and I was given an office in the continuing education department in another building. This arrangement was not conducive to my making changes for improving student success – understandably, students couldn't find where we were located. The next year I was allotted three small rooms in the math department: one for a part-time secretary (which I didn't have), one for advising and one for me.

Thus with three little rooms, one phone and one lamp and neither furniture nor a secretary, I got an advisement center started. There were several applicants for the secretarial position. The person I chose said she didn't know much about computers but was willing to learn. Her sister, on the other hand was a computer guru and secretary in the business department. Further, this woman/ applicant was sweet-natured – a characteristic I thought necessary for dealing with confused/failing students. Choosing Adele to be my secretary was one of the best decisions I ever made. Another professor whose office was across the hall from my new office was a successful writer of many federally funded math projects. He was looking for a part-time secretary also. So Adele was positioned in an office given to me for advising but served as part-time secretary to my math colleague.

The honors program, by now, had taken off and it became difficult for me to manage honors as well as advising. The provost and I met. He said, "It's going to be necessary for you to choose which program you will be able to continue to direct." I answered, "The honors program is now well established and on its way. I need to stay with the advising program." He showed me figures indicating

---

13   RhoGam – an immunoglobulin drug administered to an RH-negative- woman who has delivered an RH-positive baby to prevent maternal anibodies from forming.

that the dropout rate of undeclared students was much lower than it had been before I started university-wide advising. He was relieved that I should stay with the advising program I had started.

It was hard work to put a respectable and professional advising program in place where we had nothing. But Adele and I put our creative energies together and invented several ways of making our operation appear professional and established. We charmed the custodian into finding some unused furniture. From the computer laboratory in the college of nursing we obtained a table that normally would feed computer paper from a box on the floor, through a slot in the table and then into a printer. Where separate sheets of paper rather than boxed paper came into use, that table was no longer useful. We were grateful to have it and put it in the little room where we did advising.

A strategy I instituted had to do with the way we kept records. Individual summaries and suggestions were written on NCR paper so we would have a copy for our files. Thus, on a subsequent visit to the advising center, we would be able to check whether the student had followed through on the advisor's recommendations. One of our rather witty advisors would end his advising session with, "OK, here's your copy of our advising session details and this copy will go in our files." Then he would pass the office copy through the computer paper slot and it would, of course, go onto the floor below. That advisor would keep a straight face and the student would just stare at the 'filed' copy on the floor and leave with a quizzical face.

I selected my faculty advisors carefully. Many college faculty members are brilliant in their academic field, have impressive research and publications but are useless when it comes to students advising. That type of person was urged to send their advisees to us.

Where we had only one phone and were not yet established to have a budget to get another phone and extension, Adele and I figured a way to make it look like we had an established operation going on. I bought a dual phone jack and a very long extension cord. We attached the cord to Adele's phone and ran the wire up the wall of her office. The both of us stood on Adele's desk and with coat hangers pulled the wire across the ceiling of the advising room and then down the wall of my office. It was then attached to the princess phone I brought in from home. When a call came in, Adele would answer, "Advising center, this is Adele, how may I help you?" "I'm Mrs. Smith. I need to talk with Dr. daMaglia about my son's academic problems." "Just a minute, I'll transfer your call." Then Adele would hustle down the hall to my door. "Pick up the phone. There is a parent on the line." This arrangement even fooled the comptroller who came by to find out how we had two phone extensions when we were registered and budgeted for one.

At course registration times, the corridors outside our offices were filled with students and there was nowhere for them to sit. Again, the custodian found a couch that he put along the wall of the main corridor. I casually told some of these advising vignettes to my mother. I can't think what kind of image she had about this uncomfortable, thinly padded metal couch. She probably thought it was a nice upholstered one. She gave me an afghan she had knit to put on it. I didn't want to reject her offer. I took it to work and put it on the couch. The very next morning I came to work to find the couch gone and the afghan on the floor. Our helpful custodian came by. "There's a couch in Professor Jay's office that wasn't there yesterday." He unlocked that professor's door and sure enough there was our couch. Adele, Adele's sister and I retrieved it and put it back in the hallway. When I confronted the professor about 'stealing' my couch, he suggested that the graduate students must have done the furniture moving the past evening. "Where did those students get a key?" He didn't answer. Adele and I chuckled about that incident many times. I made her promise never to tell my mother how her afghan was tossed on the floor during the 'couch caper.'

Some students were a challenge to advise. On a Thursday morning before a Labor Day weekend, I received a call from a woman who was stepmother to a guy named Clayton. She lived in New Jersey and informed me she had just packed up the car and sent Clayton on his way to us to get registered for fall classes. He had been accepted on a provisional basis. "I'll be on the lookout for him," I told her. Later in the day, Clayton called asking, "Where are you located on campus?"

"Where are you?"

"I'm in the library."

"OK. Look out the windows that face the center of the campus. See the building across the way with red drapes? Go to the third floor of that building. I'm in the math department."

He never showed up.

The next day (the Friday before Labor Day weekend) at 3:30 P.M. Clayton appeared looking like hell.

"Where have you been?" I asked him.

"I couldn't find you."

"But where have you been?"

"In my car – I slept there."

"Oh my, well let's quickly put together a course schedule for you and get you registered." I looked at his pathetic transcript of a year of study at his previous school. He had few transferable credits; so I began to develop a basic liberal arts set of classes for him: English 102, Economics 101, Math 101, and History 101. He said, "I don't need Economics 101 because I had it at my last school."

"Yes, but you got a D and that won't transfer."

"But I already learned all that stuff."

"Not if you got a D."

"OK, then."

Then I asked if he had hobbies or interests that we could consider for choosing an elective. He said he loved to sing and had an excellent voice. I explained that I couldn't enroll him in a voice class without having an audition.

"Are you able to read music?"

"Of course."

Fortunately there was a voice instructor available in the music department and I sent Clayton right over for an audition. With that done, I closed up the advising center and left for the holiday weekend.

The Tuesday after the holiday, Clayton was at the door when I arrived at my office. "What's up?" I asked him.

"I need a different elective."

"Why? What happened to taking voice?"

"I didn't pass my audition."

"How come?"

"It turns out I don't know how to read music. I couldn't sing the piece they gave me."

Apparently, Clayton must have done acceptable academic work because I met up with him a year and a half later and he was still enrolled. He was coming around the corner eating a chocolate candy bar. I said, "Hi Clayton. How are you doing?"

"Do I know you?"

"You should. I'm the one who set up your first set of classes here."

"Wow! What a good memory you have."

Fact is – how could you forget a guy like Clayton?

Another student used to bring his grandfather with him when he came to the advising center. This old man kept interrupting saying, "I'm eighty-five years old. I'm Russell's grandfather." After he said that several times, I just ignored him. Funny thing is that when he came back a year later, he was still repeating the same lines. I wanted to ask, "Shouldn't you be eighty-six by now?"

A few of our students were in motorized wheel chairs. I couldn't get them into my office or the advising room when we were in the math department because the doorways were too narrow. Therefore, I had to advise these students in the corridor where there was no privacy. I knew that was wrong and probably illegal.

At last I got my big chance. There was a substantial change of administrators. The provost moved on and the dean of business was appointed to that position temporarily. And we had a new president who had formally been the head of a military school. I waited until he was about eight weeks into the position and made an appointment to see him. Someone suggested that to communicate with military types, you best limit your information to one sheet of paper and bullet your main points. Maybe military people live an urgent life style and don't have time for unnecessary words. So my bullets addressed the craziness of our advising center facilities, the illegality of what we were doing to students in wheel chairs and the huge improvement in retention we had accomplished with undeclared students and those in transition between majors. The president said, "Thank you. I'll look into all this." He expected me to get up and leave. I didn't. I said, "That's not good enough. I'm not leaving until you offer something more substantive. Please don't say you'll put it in the hands of the provost. He's only temporary and I've been here long enough to know that nothing will happen. You will each think the other is doing something about the situation."

"Well what do you want?" asked the president.

"A real advising center with wide doors and a conference room for advisor training and student group advising."

"OK. I'll get this problem solved. I'll take care of it personally. But please don't come back and ask for anything else. By the way, I see you being a college president yourself someday!"

Shortly after that conference, I was asked to meet with some architectural engineers to design an advising center. The president moved the print shop to another location and designated all that space to be used for university academic advising. I'm not an architect, but here's the amateur floor plan I made and submitted for the new center. I only knew how to draw lines for walls and how and where to indicate doorways.

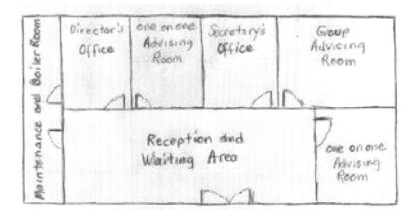

Carpeting was installed and furniture was sent out for reupholstering to match the carpet. We were given second hand desks that came from a registry of vehicles office.

somewhere. (The reason I knew that was where they came from was because RMV stickers would fall out of my desk whenever I slammed the drawer.

There was only one minor problem with our new 'digs.' My desk was up against a door in the wall that led to the boiler room for the building. There was another door at the end of the reception area that went to the same boiler room area. On a few occasions, I would be sitting at my desk and a workman would open the door not expecting to find an office there. One time, the guy even started to climb over my desk. "Excuse me; can't you use that other door?" "Oh, I didn't know there was one over there." I had to wonder – how did he get in there if he didn't know how to get out?

As stated earlier, I selected advisors for the center very carefully. They had to be laid-back, gentle with students' feelings, knowledgeable about university requirements and patient. The center became a place where faculty advisors would come even when they weren't 'on duty' just to relax. For some reason we were always laughing about something. For example, Professor Jerry P. was getting ready to advise a student. He asked Adele to get the file. The student's name was Lau, he said. Adele searched the files and couldn't find anyone with that name. She asked, "How are you spelling that?"

"LAU," he answered.

"Oh, Jerry – that's an abbreviation for Liberal Arts Undeclared – that's not his name!"

One of our advisors, Murray, was a curmudgeon – old fashioned, and set in his ways. He'd been teaching at the university for at least one hundred years. In spite of all that, he was a lovable kind of guy and we teased him all the time. He came to the advising center every morning wearing a straw hat (weather permitting) and carrying his cup of coffee. Most everyone knew I made most of my own clothes and Murray, being a bachelor, decided to take advantage of my sewing talent. He brought me his mending. Most often he presented me with a pair of pants that had a split seam in the crotch. Finally, I told him, "Murray, if you wouldn't fart so much, I wouldn't have to do so much sewing for you." At my retirement party, the advisors did a 'roast.' In the program, Murray came walking out from behind a curtain wearing his straw hat, carrying his coffee mug and a plastic bag. I exclaimed, "Oh God, here's Murray being Murray." When he approached me, he took a pair of pants out of the bag and handed them to me. I held them up to the audience and said, "Look. The holes are always in the crotch!"

We finally had a nice, pleasant and welcoming academic advising center established. At one of my routine visits to the doctor, my blood pressure was high. "Do you have a lot of pressure on you at work?" he asked. "Not really," I replied. In retrospect, I realize that I had taken on a lot of responsibility to implement plans to improve student retention. The freshman year is a difficult time for college students – so many have trouble adjusting to the demands and independence of that first year away from home. To make a smoother transition, I pre-registered most entering students into a class schedule that included one course where the professor would serve as the student's academic advisor. To accomplish that I had to find suitable professors who would be willing to take on this role. It seemed like I was always calling up colleagues asking for favors: "I know your 'intro' course is full, but would you please take one more student?" "Would you advise another group of twenty –five students?" "Would you please review this student's study abroad schedule to be sure it will meet his/her graduation requirements?" One political science professor would always reply, "How could I say no to the Queen of England?" At my retirement party I was referred to as the Mother Teresa of the university.

I went 'to bat' for many students who were about to be dismissed from the university for unsatisfactory academic performance. I would ask, "Do you really want to be here?" If they said yes, I had them sign a contract with me and the dean of their college obligating them to see me every two weeks. They had to make study sheets per my directions and then show them and their exam results to me at each session. It didn't take a whole semester before they had themselves turned around and didn't need to see me anymore. They had learned a method of studying that worked. The success stories regarding the students who came to the advising center gradually became known around the campus and more and more departments wanted to send their students to us.

The state offered an early retirement incentive plan. The objective was to get older, tenured faculty off the state payroll and then hire younger and fewer faculty for less money. My previous work as a nurse at a state hospital combined with my years at the university and my age qualified me for this retirement opportunity and I took it. As my retirement date approached, I came to realize that my efforts had been noticed and appreciated campus-wide. The Faculty Senate voted to present me with the first Yvette Sampson Award for my 'understanding treatment' of students.

The Council of Academic Deans nominated me for a "National Student Advocate Award." I was chosen and went to the University of South Carolina to receive this honor. While there I was asked to present a workshop where I detailed "Maglia's Methods" for starting and building good programs for students. (See Appendix B.)

The graduating class also honored me at their awards banquet. A partial text of that presentation is in Chapter 11.

Most exciting of all was the retirement party that was given to me. It was at a country club where several buffet stations were set up. There was a band and about 150 people in attendance – faculty, administrators, secretaries and even the custodian, who brought his family. The advisors 'roasted' me and I laughed so hard and so much, I thought my face would crack. Then I offered my retirement speech telling what I planned to do in retirement things like: play my organ more often (the one with the keys and pedals), raise kabuki mushrooms and go to Italy and drive the Italians 'pazzia' (that's crazy) with my university style of Italian. When I practiced speaking Italian with my mother-in-law, she would sometimes say, "Basta (enough!) Giulia. You're giving me a headache." I had to keep stopping during my presentation to wait for the audience to stop laughing.

It was the largest and most entertaining retirement party given to any faculty member before or since. At one point, the band started playing "A Pretty Girl is Like a Melody," and a stream of people came out from behind the curtain wearing the scarves, hats and purses I had made to match some of the outfits I had sewn for myself. It took a moment for me to recognize my own accessories. "Hey, wait, those are my clothes!" I shouted. (The party organizers had met my husband somewhere to get hold of all that stuff.)

I left the university 'on top of my game' and 'on a high' and never looked back.

Now, in my retirement years, it's as if I have yet another career – teaching knitting and selling my own knitted creations. (See Chapter 9.) I think that will be it. Oh, I forgot – perhaps I should write a book.

CHAPTER 7

My Own Family

BEN

My son Ben turned out to be a hell-of-a nice guy. Never would I have bet on that when he was a kid. He let me know even before he was born that he would always do things his way. My due date was the nineteenth of May, but Ben decided not to arrive until two and a half weeks later. For some reason, I had a romantic notion that my labor would start at night. I went to bed each evening after the nineteenth of May expecting to experience some signs of immanent labor. Such anticipation prevented me from getting a restful night's sleep. In the morning, discovering that I was still pregnant, I would spend the day tired, frustrated and moping around, only to start the cycle again that evening.

When labor finally did start, it was early in the morning of June fourth. My husband dropped me off at the hospital on his way to work. (Fathers were not allowed or expected to participate in labor and delivery at that time.) Again, Ben made labor difficult. He was coming down the birth canal so that the back of his head was against the tail of my spine rather than his face. Each contraction painfully pushed his large, bony head against my spine and the position of his head took more time to mold and move down the birth canal. A nurse friend of mine massaged the bottom of my back to relieve the pressure until my skin was raw. For several days after delivery the skin on my back side would burn when I splashed Jean Nate cologne on myself after a shower.

After being in labor for twelve hours, the obstetrician took me into the delivery room, administered general anesthesia and I then woke to greet a red-headed, over nine pound baby boy. I was disappointed that I couldn't have had a more natural childbirth, but was relieved that labor was over and I had a healthy baby. Except for some episodes of colic, Ben was a happy baby. I'd always have a project to do while he napped and it always seemed like he'd wake sooner than I planned. But when I opened the door to his room, he'd jump up and down with excitement – his droopy, wet diaper hanging down – and be so happy to see me. With that loving welcome, I forgot what I was trying to accomplish and greeted him with equal enthusiasm. Ben walked early – at nine months- and never stopped running after that. He could not accept being placed in a playpen because it was too confining - ditto about his crib. It may sound cruel, but for his safety, I had to put a harness on him when he went to bed at night. It was fastened to the far side of his crib so he could stand up and walk around the bed, but he could not climb out and roam about the house at night. His harness was accepted as part of his bedtime ritual along with bathing and reading. If I forgot to put on the harness, he would remind me saying, "Arnice?"

Thinking I could help Ben become an early reader, I made little signs with the names of things around the house and attached them to each appropriate item. STOVE was on the stove and LAMP was on the lamp, etc. Ben took them all down and had lots of fun sticking each name card into the tiny space between the stove and kitchen cabinets.

Ben laughed and giggled a lot and had a better than average vocabulary for a toddler or a preschooler. He was truly a free spirit and enjoyed talking – a lot! I asked him once what would happen when the new baby came along and should want to say something. Ben said, "We'll have to tell the new baby to be quiet."

Riding on an elevator once, he asked what sperm was. Everyone was smiling as I offered the standard explanation about the seed from a man that can make a baby. Before I could go any further, he asked, "What has that got to do with whales?"

I enrolled Ben in an art course at the local YMCA. One lesson had to do with drawing pine trees with chalk, developing them from triangles one on top of another. Then the instructor suggested that these budding artists draw an animal somewhere among the trees. Ben drew an elephant. When she saw that she asked, "Do we normally see elephants where pine trees grow?" She assumed Ben would rub out the elephant and put in a mouse or some other animal one would find in the forest. When she came around again, she saw that the elephant was still in the picture. She asked why he hadn't made any changes. Ben told her that he had made up a name for his picture. It would be entitled, "The Lost Elephant."

Ben had just turned two when my husband took a summer job at a boy's camp. The swimming instructor was giving a lesson to the campers on the beach when he saw Ben jump off the end of the pier nearby. He blew the whistle to get the campers out of the water so he could run over and rescue Ben. I was on the pier and shouted, "Not to worry, he's swimming!" Ben swam like a frog underwater, all the way to the shallow end, stood up, and got back on the pier ready to repeat his accomplishment all over again. I thought we'd have to do CPR on the WSI (water safety instructor).

The next summer we visited an aunt and uncle who had a yacht on Lake Michigan. After leaving the dock and motoring some distance, my uncle dropped anchor where we could swim and enjoy lunch on board. Ben immediately jumped overboard and started swimming. My aunt nearly had a heart attack and was sputtering something incoherent. My cousin watched Ben swimming around and calmly suggested we put down a ladder so Ben could climb back on board when he was ready. On the yacht was a glass ashtray which sat in a cork bowl. Ben must have thought it looked like something to eat and he took a huge bite out of the cork. My aunt has kept that ashtray and its tooth marked cork all these forty-some years. We decided to wrap it up and give it to him for Christmas this year.

When it was time for Ben to start public school, I had had my second child – a daughter named Trudy. Where she was just a baby, I looked forward to Ben going off to school and his being out of my hair for a few hours each day. He was full of energy and he tried my patience at times. For example, I had been talking on the kitchen phone one morning when Ben came by carrying what looked like chunks of black construction paper. I went into the play room to discover that Ben had pulled off the front frame of the TV and then disconnected the speaker. Today there is nothing Ben can't fix or do mechanically or otherwise. Perhaps that was the beginning of his learning how things work. Another time I had bought a three-foot, true blue spruce tree (the kind that stays blue all year round.) It was quite expensive. I planted it with tender, loving care over a bed of fish guts for fertilizer. After the job was done, Ben decided to jump over it. I explained, "Don't do that because you might break the leader branch and the tree won't grow into its correct shape." He jumped over it again. "Don't do that I said. Don't do it again." He did it again and broke the leader branch. At that moment the tree was worth more to me than Ben's life! I gave him a solid spanking. (It's embarrassing to remember that now.)

When Ben stepped on the school bus for the first time all eager for adventure, he immediately faced a set of rules: sit down, face forward, don't stand until the bus is at a complete stop, etc. "Oh, oh," I thought, "School for Ben is going to be like pushing a square peg through a round hole." And until fourth grade that was the case. I didn't look forward to parent/teacher conferences where I had to listen to examples of his not following the rules, wanting to do things his way and always having an answer. Ben came home from first grade one day with one of his Thomas heeled,

Stride Rite shoes missing. Where his class had had recess late in the afternoon, he wore his sneakers home. "Where's your other shoe?" "Oh, I remember now. We were playing basketball with my shoe using the trash can as a basket. When the bell rang, I hurried to get in line for the bus and my shoe got left in the wastebasket." I called the school custodian. He had just finished a dump run after having emptied all the classroom baskets. So much for an expensive pair of shoes. What can you do with just one?

In arithmetic, he was asked to use pencil so he could erase and correct mistakes. He insisted on using ink because, "I don't make mistakes." One teacher had him tested for academic competency. She said with his vocabulary she doubted he had a learning problem, but sent him to a specialist just in case. He proved to be substantially above grade average and Ben said all that testing was fun and he'd like to take more tests. He wouldn't back down for anyone including the school principal, telling him, "I don't have to do (whatever it was) because my father is a teacher and you can call him if you want to."

Then in fourth grade everything changed. He got Miss Cottrill for a teacher. She was young and pretty and Ben liked the way she tossed back her long blonde hair. He was in love with her. Miss Cottrill had a teaching style that suited Ben's approach to learning. At our first parent/teacher conference that year, I couldn't believe my ears. Is Miss Cottrill really talking about Ben or does she have us confused with someone else's parents? "What a joy it is to have Ben in my class. He is an independent learner. He takes on projects and sees them through to every last detail. Over there on the shelf is his latest science project." It had happened that on our way home from up-state New York, a bee got caught between the wiper and windshield and died there. Ben wanted to keep it for study purposes. I never thought anything more about it. But there on the shelf Miss Cottrill pointed to was a poster depicting all the parts and functions of the bee. She said he dissected the bee and examined all the parts under a microscope. That's also the year Ben became an avid reader – one Hardy Boys' mystery after another.

Then he moved onto *The Lord of the Rings* and *The Leather Stocking Tales* by Cooper.

We moved to a lovely seaside community after Ben's fourth grade where we had private beach rights. Ben had his own row-boat/skiff which he called NAPOLI (because that was the name of the boat the Hardy Boys had). He was fishing on the water almost every day and he had a good head on his shoulders when it came to "water smarts." A rather large boat yard was at the end of our street – about five houses away. In his teen years, he worked there summers driving the launch boat. People with yachts would need to be brought to their boats via the launch. At the end of a day of boating, the yachters would blow a horn requesting the launch to come get them and their belongings and bring them back to the pier. At home, I could hear that horn and think to myself, "There goes Ben." One family suffered an emergency of some kind at sea. They called in and Ben was at their mooring waiting for them when they arrived. 911 had already been called and Ben got them to the dock immediately. He told them, "Don't worry, I'll tidy and close up the craft for you." He was rewarded with a nice tip for his sensitive actions during their crisis.

Eventually, Ben acquired a twelve-foot motor boat and obtained a student permit to trap lobsters. (He was allowed twelve pots and his catch had to be for personal consumption.) The local fish market saved their gurrie for Ben to use as bait. (Lobsters are scavengers!) On a good lobstering day, we might end up with a half dozen lobsters in the refrigerator. In fact, one morning, I opened the fridge and a lobster was hanging down clinging to the egg tray. Once we ate lobsters for breakfast.

There must be folks walking around who have more than their share of genes for singing well, because I didn't get any. Neither did Ben. Worse yet, he doesn't connect with a beat or rhythm. For example, if you should beat out rat-a-tap-tap-tap, his would come out tap-a-rat-a-tap-a-rat. When students were choosing a musical instrument to play in elementary school (about fifth or sixth grade), Ben wanted to try the drums. A neighbor advised,

"Don't spend money on drums. He can start off with drum pads and sticks. You can have the ones my son left behind years ago." Ben played real drums at school with other members of the marching band. Prior to a Memorial Day celebration when the band was scheduled to play in the town's parade, Mr. Cleff called pleading for me to find a way to keep Ben home from the parade. He said Ben's drum playing had no regular beat and hindered the marching steps of the other kids. In other words, "Ben was a drummer with a different (irregular) beat." For Memorial Day my husband got tickets to a major league baseball game for himself and Ben. When we presented this opportunity, Ben said, "But Mr. Cleff is counting on me to be at the parade." " OK, I'll write a note to him explaining the situation. Hopefully, he won't be too disappointed." When he read the note, Mr. Cleff said to Ben, "Good for you. I wish I were going with you." Reading this book will be the first Ben will have heard of this subterfuge.

Ben's swearing got on my nerves. I sat him down for a heart-to-heart discussion. "I'm fucking sick and tired of your fucking God damn language. Do you come from a fucking pig pen? Do your parents talk such a dirty, God dam, fucking language? Do you have no decent vocabulary that you must always say fuck this and fuck that all the time? Do you like to hear your mother speak in such a lousy, fucking way? There will be no more of your low-down, fucking language in this house. Do you understand?" Before he could answer, Trudy came into the room and asked, "Is that it?" She had been around the corner and heard my whole tirade. She thoroughly enjoyed it.

Believe it or not, Ben was a faithful church-goer. On Easter Sunday morning, he would get up, and ride his bicycle to sunrise service at the light house and be back in bed before the rest of us were awake. Our church had a fabulous minister. Nothing the kids would say or do could get a rise out of him. He treated the members of the youth group as if they were full-fledged, adult members of the church. Rev. Peters took Ben's off the wall comments and actions in stride because, as he told me, "Ben is simply a late bloomer."

At one youth group meeting there was a discussion about abortion and when does life begin. At what fetal age, if any, is abortion acceptable? Ben's answer was "Up until age thirteen." When I heard about that comment, I thought to myself, "If that were the case does Ben realize he might not be here?" The youth group went on annual retreats arranged by Rev. Peters. One year the agenda focused on the amount of care and constant supervision a baby requires. To drive that point home, each member was to care for a raw egg for the weekend; to see that the egg (baby) was protected from damage. The message was supposed to be, "Prevent pregnancy until you're ready and able to provide 24/7 care for a dependent creature." Ben wrapped his egg in gauge and adhesive tape and hid it between the rafters in the camp's bunkhouse. Then he amused himself by breaking other people's eggs when he had the chance. Only recently did he inform me that he took a Tupperware container of Jim Beam on that retreat. I fervently hope he didn't offer any to Rev. Peters.

Unrelated to church activities, Ben went on "survival" with his junior high school class. All the students were to hike up the side of a mountain, camp out and live off nature's bounty which included the stems of cat-and-nine tails, frogs, etc. Ben was perfectly happy eating what nature offered. (He claims that the pot of soup had only one frog in it, some greens and lots of packages of dried soup.) But many balked at the available menu. Ben came to the rescue. He had carried packets of peanut butter crackers and Oreo cookies in his backpack and happily sold them for one dollar each to his fellow classmates. He survived easily that weekend and made quite a profit in the process.

Ben wasn't too smart about choosing friends. For some reason, he was attracted to boys who were trouble makers and Ben would sometimes be caught 'holding the bag.' On one occasion Ben's friend, who was sitting next to him on the bus, handed Ben a lighted firecracker. To avoid injury, Ben quickly tossed it out the school bus window. That infraction was supposed to have given him a three day suspension from school. As parents, we thought suspension was not a punishment, but a reward. Ben's father went to the police chief to arrange a suitable punishment that would provide service to the town and keep Ben in school. An agreement was made between the school principal and the police chief for Ben to donate a specified number of hours doing such tasks as sweeping the side of the road leading to the town dump. Ben tried to keep his back to the road so residents arriving at the dump might not recognize him. You couldn't not know who he was with his height and the color of his hair. The dentist who lived next door returned from a dump run and commented, "Your Ben is such a hard worker. I saw him sweeping and tidying one of the town roads this morning." He had no idea that this 'hard work' was punishment for Ben. It turns out that after sweeping for a short while, the caretaker of the dump invited Ben to the maintenance shed and together they looked at *Hustler* magazines. Later the police chief had Ben moving the police cars, forgetting he wasn't yet old enough to drive.

For a short while, Ben had a paper route. On Sundays the calls came in from subscribers on his route complaining that the advertisement sections were missing from their papers. When asked, Ben explained, "That stuff is too heavy to lug around. I threw them all away." Being a paper boy was not a long-term job for Ben. Another complaint from neighbors had to do with Ben driving the motorized go-cart he built from scratch along the streets where we lived. Vehicles with motors have to be registered.

Oftentimes, I blamed myself for all the scrapes Ben got himself into. Had I failed as a parent? Did I not teach the rules of society? There were two events that gave me hope that he at least had a heart under that wild and unpredictable exterior. We had friends who owned a gas station, donut shop and corner store in a neighboring state. Everyone in that family worked various jobs in their establishment. They agreed to employ and board Ben for the summer between his sophomore and junior years of high school. We went to visit him on one of his days off and went shopping at a nearby mall. Ben wanted to buy me an outfit – a pinstriped skirt and matching jacket. When I protested, he said, "I'm working now. I'd like to buy you something." I was so touched, I cried on the way home. The following summer, Ben worked for an appliance store moving refrigerators, TVs, etc from a warehouse and delivering them to customers – sometimes on the third floor of a tenement building. As he drove the truck on his routes, he noticed a gal selling flowers on a street corner. Each time he went by it seemed to Ben that she hadn't sold anything. So, on his last trip of the day, he stopped and bought a red rose. He brought it home to me explaining that he wanted to help the poor girl out. I was touched. It didn't matter that it wasn't bought specially for me because it let me see that kindness did exist in my son's heart.

Ben was accepted at an out-of-state university that offered a unique major – marine engineering. Where he did well in math and had personal knowledge of the ocean including fish, boats, tides, etc, I thought marine engineering would be the perfect course of study for him. I was excited about his prospects – picturing him doing such things as directing the operation of an oil spill cleanup. When I went to visit him at college, I noticed he was signed up for all kinds of extracurricular activities which were posted on the dormitory's bulletin board. Also, he had redesigned his dorm room so that it was the envy of the other residents. The bed was bolted high up on the wall so that his desk fit underneath it. As a result, his room had plenty of room for 'horsing around.' Trudy didn't like visiting her brother. She said that dorm smelled like feet and farts.

Over the holidays after one semester of college, Ben's grade report arrived: all Fs except for a C in English. "No more college for you until you can be more responsible. Go back to delivering refrigerators and see it that's what you want to do for the rest of your life."

At about that same time I had done a load of the family's laundry and was distributing the clean clothes to everyone's rooms. In Ben's closet was an unusual sight: a sleeping bag hung over the clothes pole and behind it a desk lamp casting its light onto a marijuana plant. I let Ben have it. "You could have set the house on fire. Your sister sleeps in the next room. Did you consider she might burn to death in her bed because of you?" He said he was taking care of the plant for a friend. "You have that plant and that setup out of here by two o'clock or you can't live here anymore." By the deadline there wasn't a trace of his botanical project.

Ben went to work full-time and rented a cottage with another guy. I decided to separate from my husband and moved out also. Eventually, Ben returned back home. I did not. Some more infractions of the law occurred. He drove his car through the fence at the town park, left it there and tried to run home before the police caught up with him. He was found hiding in some bushes and made to pay for damages. (I suspect he was drunk.) A friend of his made a claim that his vehicle was stolen. Instead it was dismantled by the owner, Ben and another guy named Vinnie. Vinnie kept the motor behind his father's shed. The other parts were stored in the garage of my former home. Vinnie decided to sell the motor and advertized it in the local paper. The vehicle identification number was checked and he was arrested for participation in insurance fraud. He squealed on the other two guys. The police found the other car parts and cited Ben. The third guy couldn't be found because he was on a fishing boat and out at sea most of the time. (Perhaps that's why he didn't need that car.) Ben and Vinnie had to hire a lawyer, go to court and pay fines and legal fees. I might never have known about any of this except that my mother read about it under "court transactions" in her newspaper. (She was after all, a legal secretary.) I'll go to my grave wondering why Ben's father didn't do anything when he saw those car parts in the garage.

Ben decided to give college another try. I enrolled him in a physics course offered evenings at the university where I taught. He did well and the following semester started day courses working toward a degree in mechanical engineering. Every day I would make his lunch and leave it in a refrigerator near my office. Because of my professorial position there, he attended college tuition free. It wasn't until his junior year that he seemed to get it all together.

He joined a study group and made the dean's list his last three semesters. No mother was prouder than I on the day of his college graduation. Like all other faculty members in attendance, I was wearing full academic regalia. When Ben's name was called, I went to stand next to the stage so I could give him a well-deserved hug as he descended the stairs with his diploma.

After a couple of engineering jobs, he landed a position with a company that manufactures specialized machine parts for vehicles and planes. He's been promoted several times and is now a plant manager responsible for machinery as well as employees who work the machines. He's happy there. It's been a good fit.

Ben had one unhappy marriage that ended in divorce. He has no children. Now, after a six year courtship, he's engaged to a super gal with grown children. He owns a home that he's remodeled top to bottom doing all the work himself. He's a perfectionist and his home is beautiful. It's only a few blocks from the town wharf and the park where he drove his car through the fence.

Ben has done thousands of jobs for me from putting up a trellis and arbor for my grapevine to finishing a special room in the basement for my sewing. He's a kind and gentle man. I think I'll keep him. I've decided not to have an abortion.

TRUDY

Like her brother, Trudy walked early – eight months. The pediatrician wondered if she might have a congenital hip. "We'll know for sure when she starts to walk."

"She already walks!"

"Put her down and let me see."

I put her down and she walked right out of the examining room.

"That settles it. She doesn't have congenital hips."

We were at a barbeque in early summer when she was nine months old. She came tottering across the lawn toward my mother. "Good gracious. How does she pull herself up to start walking on this grass?" You had to see it to believe it. She started on her knees, straightened out one leg in front, rolled onto that leg, got the foot of the other leg on the ground along with both hands and brought herself upright.

When she was almost two, I planned to enroll in a master's degree program. With this pending change in routine, I reasoned it would not be a good idea to start toilet training. That project could wait a year. The potty chair was in the bathroom however and one day, during the Labor Day weekend, Trudy walked into the kitchen without her diaper and said, "Pee, pee." Sure enough, a dry diaper was on the floor and pee, pee was in the potty. She trained herself. What a gift!

I had the scare of my life one afternoon. I was in the den reading the newspaper when I suddenly realized the house was very quiet. The usual sounds and noises of Trudy were absent. I called to her, but there was no answer. Did she walk out the door while I was behind the newspaper? I ran outside and up and down the street calling her. Had she been kidnapped? I was panicky. I went back into the house to collect my thoughts. There on the stairs was the doll she had been playing with. Upstairs I found her — sound asleep in her crib. She had climbed in there by herself. She was a smart cookie.

When Trudy started preschool she was nearly the youngest in her class having been born toward the end of the year. Early on, the students were tested for academic readiness and aptitude. The teacher was surprised to find Trudy at the top of the scale in spite of her being younger than most of the other kids.

I hired a neighbor, Mrs. Barnes to get Trudy on and off the school bus on the days I worked. Mrs. Barnes lived about twelve houses away and she had three children who were around high school and junior high school age. She told me that Trudy could remember a long list of tasks to be done – far more than her own three children put together. With birthday money Trudy wanted to buy a toy ironing board and iron. She set it up in the aisle of the toy store and pretended to be ironing. Normally, I don't iron.

If it's fabric that needs ironing, I don't wear it. So Trudy could only be imitating Mrs. Barnes. Frankly, I don't think Trudy irons today either. Her stuff comes out of the dryer, gets folded and put away. Her imitation of Mrs. Barnes didn't last a lifetime.

One day the school bus made its usual stop in front of Mrs. Barnes' house but Trudy wasn't among the children getting off.

"Where's Trudy?"

"She got off at her house."

"Today's Wednesday. She's supposed to get off here. Why did you let her off at her house? There's nobody home there. Why am I wasting my time talking to you? I've got to go find her."

So Mrs. Barnes went tearing down the street yelling, "Don't worry, Trudy, Mrs. Barnes is coming." She got to my house and there was no Trudy there either. She sat on the front steps to catch her breath and wonder what Trudy might think to do where no one was home. She remembered Trudy talking about the lady across the street who had a new baby she would like to see. So she went to the neighbor's and there she found Trudy sitting at the kitchen table eating Jell-O and chatting away with the baby's mother.

Trudy started first grade in the seaside community we had moved to. Our neighborhood was full of children Trudy's age and you never saw her but what she was in a pack of happy, wholesome friends; both boys and girls. She, too, had a small boat with a two HP motor. It was named, "The Ruby." Whenever I needed to catch up with Trudy in the summers I would simply go down to our neighborhood beach. There she'd be with a bunch of friends – some in the boat and some swimming around it. "Hey Trudy, get back here. We're gonna be late for your orthodontist appointment." She'd hop out of the boat and swim to shore while the other kids eventually dragged the boat up onto the dunes. There were always adult neighbors on the beach. Trudy and her buddies knew they were not to go in the water or take out the boat if there were no adults present. If they did, the boat would be taken away.

At an early age Trudy was an entrepreneur. One of my neighbors told how Trudy had picked the flowers from her garden and then went to her door, rang the bell and offered to sell the lady her own flowers. At school in the winter time, the students piled snow into a huge hill which they then slid down on pieces of cardboard. Trudy was at the bottom of the hill selling cocoa. The teacher said Trudy had the cocoa in a cooler. I have no idea how she pulled that off.

Trudy took organ lessons and when older studied the oboe. She played the prelude on the church organ one Sunday. It was Clare de Lune by Debussy. The organ was located in a loft area at the back of the church. The parishioners facing forward are unable to see the organist. There was Trudy at age nine playing the organ in church. There I sat in my pew with goose bumps that nearly reached the ceiling. Her performance was perfect and beautiful. The oboe didn't go as well. I thought it would be great if she could master the oboe. I had heard that colleges and universities with a respectable music programs would award full scholarships to any decent oboist they could get their hands on. I now understand why. To play the oboe one has to take a deep breath and then blow air through a narrow reed; something like trying to blow through a strand of hair. The oboist has to hold that breath for a long time- until one feels like his/her head is going to explode. That instrument goes through reeds a mile a minute and a dedicated oboist must learn to make their own reeds or go broke. On top of all these difficulties, our dog couldn't stand the sounds of Trudy's oboe. He would stand beside her and try to out-howl her playing. You would think an intelligent Welsh corgi would go someplace else when hearing her practice rather than park himself right next to her. We eventually deep sixed the oboe.

Prior to her sixteenth birthday, I decided to make Trudy a small memory quilt. I sent a note to all the people who were in her life asking each one to draw a picture or write a message in a four by four box. These were transferred to the squares in the quilt by embroidery or appliqué. There were also squares of fabric from the drapes I had made for the living room and den. Trudy says that every time she looks at it she sees something she didn't notice before.

Trudy's claim to fame in high school was her prowess on the basketball court and the track and field arena. Rarely could anyone get by her to shoot a basket. She kept the opposing team's score to a minimum and had a huge role to play in taking her team to the state finals. Unfortunately, she was knocked down during the final match and suffered a sprained ankle. The team lost their bid to make it to the top.

There's still a plaque on the wall at her high school for setting a record in the discus and shot put. She qualified for the Junior Olympics in St. Louis. Getting on the plane with a shot put in her luggage caused quite a commotion. Security personnel gathered all around wondering what to do with that "bomb" that was in her carryon. She took third place in the shot put. "Where's your medal?" I asked her as she got off the plane returning home.

"I thought you'd be wearing it."

"How did you know I won a medal?"

"I read about it in the paper."

"The medal is in my suitcase."

Trudy's upper arms were quite muscular and large from participating in these events. We went shopping for a prom dress. In the changing room I heard a rip. "Mom, I can't get my arm in or out of this dress." That was the case with all the other garments she tried on. I'm afraid we left J.C. Penney with several dresses that had torn sleeves. We went to a fabric store and picked out some pretty material and I made a gown with wide enough sleeves.

Understandably, her love of sports and the encouragement of her coaches and mentors, led her to apply to a university as a physical education major. It was a beautiful campus, but over a six hour trip to get there. She left behind a boyfriend, Fred, who went into the service. Coming home at Christmas break she announced she and Fred were engaged. I was sorely disappointed because in my eyes, this Fred was a loser and going nowhere.

There are plenty of stories about how a parent's disapproval of a boyfriend might drive the couple even closer together to unite against criticism. I didn't want to risk that chance. Hiding my disappointment, I simply said, "That Fred certainly has good taste!" Over semester break she wanted to go with Fred when he returned to his military base out west. For a Christmas present, I gave her a round-trip ticket to go there. It may have been the smartest thing I ever did; for sometime later the engagement was off. Trudy informed me over coffee in a diner that Fred was indeed a loser. This was my opportunity to state my case.

"I'm glad the engagement is off. May I now whisper some words of advice in your ears? Don't go for looks. Looks don't last. Go for brains. Go for someone who has ambition; someone who will likely earn a good salary and provide a comfortable life style for you and your future family." She said she understood what I was saying.

Trudy did well academically. Where she was such a long distance away, I wasn't privy to what extra-curricular fun she was having except for one story. She and her roommate bought an artificial Christmas tree at a large box store for their dorm room which they decorated with tinsel and ornaments. When exams were over and it was time to head home for the semester break, they boxed up the tree and returned it to the store for a refund. However, they didn't bother to remove the tinsel. Trudy still chuckles today thinking about the next customer who bought that tree and discovered it was already decorated.

Somewhere along the way Trudy was reconnected with a fellow who had been just a friend when they were in junior high school. His name was Jim and he was attending a university in our home state. It's interesting that where I was, at that time, a faculty advisor helping other parents' children to successfully meet academic requirements, I should get a call from Trudy's advisor.

He said, "I have Trudy here in front of me and she has love in both eyes. She wants to finish her degree requirements at the university where Jim is studying. I will help her design a plan that transfers courses from there to here so she will get her degree from this university." I was so pleased that someone was doing for my daughter what I had been doing for others. Sure enough, she earned her diploma and had the school send it to me.

Trudy married Jim whose work as an engineer took the two of them to several states before they settled in Michigan. She took a job as a recruiter (head hunter) and loved every minute of it. When I was receiving radiation therapy for breast cancer (Chapter 10), she took a week off to stay with me and drive me for my treatments. She asked me to remind her how to knit and we started a pair of mittens. Sometime after she returned home she called to let me know she'd sent a package. She wouldn't say what it was. I assumed it might be the mittens with a dropped stitch or some other knitting problem. Several days went by with no package in my mailbox. But she kept calling to ask if it had come yet. "Why would she be so concerned about that parcel if it's just mittens?" I wondered. Finally, she had to explain, "I'm pregnant and what I sent you was something to let you know that." The next day I waited for the mail carrier to ask what could have happened to my package. She said it was in the holding box and she wondered why I hadn't taken it out. "But you never left a key in my box for me to know it was there. My daughter sent me something to announce she is pregnant with my first grandchild."

"Oh, I'm so excited for you." And the mail lady gave me a big hug. She was so happy for me that I couldn't be angry with her for not leaving that key. In the package was a Mary Engelbreit cup and saucer decorated with an Italian proverb: "When a child is born, so is a grandmother." How thrilling and touching that was.

Trudy tracked me and my husband down on the golf course while we were vacationing in Florida. She said her blood work had come back with an unusually high level of Human Gonadatropin which indicated either a problem with the pregnancy or a multiple pregnancy. She was scheduled for an ultrasound the next day. "Oh Trudy, for sure it'll turn out to be twins. My mother had twins, my aunt had twins. We apparently are a family of females who produce multiple eggs each month. Call me tomorrow and let me know what the ultrasound shows." Dutifully, she called to tell me she was carrying twins – two boys. "How do they know they are boys so soon?" "Because they were both presenting a crotch view!"

Although she had names picked out for them, she referred to them as Baby A and Baby B. So I started calling them Alphonse and Bartholomew. Tired of hearing that, she revealed the two names. Baby A would be Harry and Baby B Will.

Prior to her estimated date of delivery, my husband I flew to Michigan to help out. Trudy was huge and had swollen ankles. She was more than ready and prepared for the big day. Her obstetrician, concerned about her blood pressure and the danger of eclampsia decided Trudy should have her labor induced. It took two days before contractions began. In the meantime, I stayed at her home and cleaned, cleaned and cleaned the house even though it didn't need it. My husband played golf.

Finally the call came. The twins had arrived and within fifteen minutes I was there to see them together in one crib. Harry weighed in at six pounds, six ounces and Will at six pounds, nine ounces. They are fraternal twins; their differences easily recognizable. The day they were born, a tornado struck the area. My husband and I didn't understand what the sirens meant. We were in a pizza parlor when we were informed that we should get home and under cover. Meanwhile, Trudy was calling Jim to see if he knew where we were. Back at their home, we got under the staircase in the basement with Jim, the dog, the cats and the kitty litter box. Jim's mother called wanting details about the babies. "You don't understand. We can't talk right now because we're under the staircase going through a tornado warning. We'll have to call you back as soon as the sirens shut down."

Trudy came home with the babies. She put them on a blanket on the den floor. Along came the family dog. He sniffed each baby and then plopped down beside them. I had the sense that the dog was saying, "OK. It'll be my job now to look after these two little guys." And that's exactly what he did. One day when they were toddlers, I was watching the two of them outdoors. I turned my back on Will to watch Harry heading for the garage. When I looked back around for Will, I couldn't see him. In a panic, I called to Trudy, who was in the house. "I don't know where Will went." "Just look where the dog is facing. There he is heading to the sand box in the next yard."

I stayed with my daughter, son-in-law and my little munchkins for another three weeks. I showed Trudy how to bathe the boys and kept them with me at night until they were both awake and hungry. Then I would take them to her to breast feed. While nursing, I would bring Trudy some juice or a fruit salad and take the babies back to my room after they were fed. In the morning, I made Trudy a healthy breakfast, played with the babies while she showered and did whatever errands she needed done. Once, she sent me to the hardware store to buy a replacement sponge for her mop. I had to make several stops before I found what she wanted. Back at the house, I happened to pass by a mirror and saw I had a big glob of mustard on my face. I was taking good care of Trudy, but presenting a messy personal appearance going here and there in her little town.

The day I was scheduled to leave and return home was very upsetting. I had become so attached to those two little guys. Trudy had adapted beautifully to her motherly role and the babies were nursing well, thriving and content. I believe new mothers need to be mothered and I gave that philosophy my full attention. The driver of the van I hired to take me to the airport tried to make flirty conversation. But I sat in the back seat with the pictures of 'my twins' crying. Trudy's mother and father-in-law arrived shortly after I left and did all kinds of things to make life easy for their son and daughter-in-law. But sometime later, Trudy dearly wanted to move closer to her family to have help with caring for her twin boys. Jim reluctantly left his job in Michigan, got work in his home state and they bought a house thirty-five minutes from me and twenty minutes from Jim's parents.

Trudy's growing up was easier on the nervous system compared to her brother, Ben. However, she was sneaky in that she would always tell me what she thought I wanted to hear rather than the truth. Finally, I can't say she was a slob; but she sure kept a messy room. This picture tells it all.

I needed to send Trudy to Girl Scout camp each summer so I could get in her room with a bulldozer and clean the place up. She never noticed that anything was missing even though I sent bags and bags of stuff to the dump.

Never did I think I might start a family tradition. When Ben and Trudy were Santa Claus believers, my mother-in-law wanted to be at our home on Christmas morning. She wanted to see the children unwrap their gifts. We kept them upstairs in one bed opening the presents in their stockings while grandma snuck into the house and waited in the living room. After the chaos of toys and wrapping paper, I went into the kitchen to make breakfast following a recipe I found in a magazine many years ago:

Sunburst Bacon Buns

1 lb sliced bacon	¼ c. light cream
4 round buns cut in half	¾ tsp salt
butter or margarine	dash pepper
6-8 beaten eggs	½ c. shredded cheddar cheese

Pan fry or broil bacon until crisp. Drain on absorbent paper. Set aside. Spread buns with margarine. Place on baking sheet. Combine eggs, cream, salt and pepper, mixing well. Cook in a small amount of margarine in medium size fry pan, stirring frequently until just set. Spoon scrambled eggs onto buttered bun halves. Allowing three slices of bacon for each bun, arrange them on top of eggs. Mound shredded cheese in center of each bun on top of bacon. Place under broiler until cheese melts.

Today I see that on Christmas mornings Trudy's boys open their stocking gifts in their beds. After the demolition of everything under the tree, Uncle Ben makes Sunburst Bacon Buns for breakfast. Perhaps this is a Christmas tradition that Will and Harry will carry on with their own families someday.

THE TWINS – HARRY and WILL

Once Trudy's family moved back here, I said I'd come to her house at least one day a week to play with the babies so she could tackle her 'to do' list. They were so much fun-alert and laughing all the time. I pushed them in their swings by the hour, sang to them and told them stories I made up while they were swinging back and forth. For example; I told about a woodpecker who tried to make a hole in an aluminum gutter, and about a bird that kept losing her nest because she built it on top of a train that would then leave the station. We sang over and over, "The Bear Went over the Mountain," except Will sang it as "The Berry over the Mountain." They seemed to appreciate my singing. But years later they say, "Don't sing, Grandma.

You are so off-key." I've been told that before, so I know they're right. Besides they have musical talent of their own. Harry plays the guitar and Will plays the organ and sings in the school choir.

All Grandmothers have their favorite stories to tell. Here are two of mine: Trudy won a cruise for herself and her husband through her business. I stayed with the twins while the parents were gone. They were about three or four. I was getting them ready for their bedtime baths. Harry was already in the tub and Will was to pee before he got in. But Will was busy watching which toys Harry was putting in the tub and not paying attention to where his urine was going. "Oh Will, watch what you're doing. You've peed all over the floor. Now you've made extra work for Grandma to clean it all up." After the bath, powdering, pj's, tooth brushing and a story, it was time for one last pass at the toilet. I reminded them, "Look at the size of that toilet bowl. Now look at the size of your penis. There's no reason why you can't manage to get all your pee into that toilet." Harry says, "But you should see Dad's penis. It's this big." He then holds up his hands about a foot apart. "Nevertheless, I imagine Dad manages to gets his pee in the toilet and not on the floor."

At age nine, I was going through the bedtime routine with them when Will announced, "The doctor says I am going through early puberty." Harry adds, "Yes, Grandma, Will has pubic hair, but I won't tell you where." "I imagine you're talking about the hair between the tops of his legs. Do either of you have any hair under your arms yet?"

They both look at their armpits. "No, not yet," says Harry, "But I have some light hairs growing on my upper lip."

For entertainment not too long ago, I suggested we eat cherries and have a contest to see who could spit the pits the furthest. Harry said there was no way he could win because Will can reach seven feet with just spit. "How far can you go," I asked. "Only two."

They are both athletic. In baseball Harry plays catcher. Never does the ball get by him. Will plays first base. The last out of the last inning of the last game this season was a play with Harry throwing the ball to Will who tagged the base before the batter / runner got there.

They are both on the student council and their report cards show an A+ in everything but art. Will says the art teacher doesn't give A+'s. Trudy must be doing something right. I never saw report cards that looked like that from my two children.

In addition they are both computer gurus. Will attended an Ivy League college one summer to study computer game design. I was amazed at how he could start with a blank screen and end up with a game on a disc that has little icons (things) running around chasing each other. He has helped me with technical details on preparing the manuscript for this book. Soon, he plans to finish some of his own writing and get something published.

Finally, Harry and Will are as different as night and day. You want a hard working, punctual guy to do a job for you? Call Harry; but be sure to have plenty of chocolate chip ice cream and choco-late syrup on hand. He will scoff down a bowl of that stuff before you've got the container of ice cream back in the freezer. You want hugs and enjoyable conversation with amazing insights? Call Will. Keep in mind Will is a carnivore. They both have a million freckles. Did I mention they are only eleven?

CHAPTER 8

MY FRIENDS—MY SISTERS

Some of the psychologists and psychiatrists mentioned in Chapter One, claim that first-borns, as opposed to later-borns, do not make lots of friends. If other first borns are like me, we are cautious about how much to reveal about ourselves to others until we discover a human being with whom "you could sit on a porch, never saying a word and walk away feeling like that was the best conversation you've ever had." (Author Unknown) In my various jobs and through teaching knitting classes, I am and have always been surrounded by wonderful and beautiful individuals. But there are some very special people in my life for whom I would give my eye teeth. No. Wait. I'd give more than that. Should any of these dear, five people: Dottie, Ella, Adele, Therese, or Penny ever need an organ transplant and I were compatible, I would hop on the operating table and tell the surgeon, "Have at it. Just be sure I'm asleep before you cut." My friendships with these women are deep and precious and my relationships with them probably say a lot about me. They are the real sisters of my life; the sisters who have stayed loyal to and caring for me through thick and thin when my own sibling sisters did not.

DOTTIE

Friendship isn't a big thing – it's a million little things.
—Author Unknown

Dottie and I became friends over a discussion of cucumber skins and reflux. We were both pregnant: Dottie with her second child and me with my first. We had joined a bowling league at the town's athletic club. Here's the way that discussion went:

Dottie: "I find when I'm pregnant, I need to leave the skins on a cucumber or I repeat."

Me: "What's repeat?"

"Repeat is to burp."

"Oh, I didn't know that. I never ate cucumbers with the skin on. I don't think they make me burp anyway."

How did a conversation like that produce a friendship that's lasted fifty years?

If I had had to pay by the minute for all the hours Dottie and I have talked on the phone, I'd be bankrupt. We lived in a small town where not much went on. We were at the same stage of development – mid twenties and child rearing. Our babies were usually down for a nap around noon time and that's when the soap opera *Days of our Lives* came on. I ate my lunch while I watched it. When it was over, Dottie would call.

"What's with that Julie?"

"She's a bitch."

"Whose baby do you think it is? Bill's or Dave's?"

"I hope Tom gets caught having that affair with Denise. Pauline doesn't deserve that kind of treatment."

It's as if we were talking about real people.

Dottie is petite. She's got an eye for fashion and puts scarves and jewelry with her outfits so that she always looks stunning. In her retirement she took a part-time job in a well-known, women's clothing store. She helps customers put garments together and quite often they leave the store having bought a piece of jewelry or other accessories they would never have thought 'went together' because Dottie points out the uniqueness or beauty of the combination. In fact, Dottie makes exquisite jewelry herself putting together unusual combinations of colorful glass and metal beads.

Dottie didn't go to college, but she is smarter than most people who did. She writes poetry and is often called upon to write and deliver a eulogy or a memorial speech. Her understanding of people's motives and behaviors is quite profound and keen. I believe her insights come from a natural common sense, some intuition and basic 'street smarts.'

She offered a clever presentation about me at a survivor's party I held eleven years after my diagnosis of cancer. Together, Dottie and her husband, Aaron started making pizzas on weekends at a local social club. That went well and led to their opening a pizza and sub shop. Next, they started up a restaurant which was attached to the sub shop. After that, they bought a lovely restaurant on a lake and made a success of that also. Wedding receptions and large parties were held there. All that responsibility, hard work and supervision of their employees was exhausting and draining- I couldn't have done it. But Dottie did and kept a sense of humor about it all.

Jokingly, I tell Dottie their success in the restaurant business was due to me. On opening day of their sub shop, it looked like they were going to run out of spaghetti sauce. Dottie called and I made a large pot of *ragu* using my own recipe and delivered it in the 'nick of time.' Of course the customers came back again and again because of that sauce.

She reminds me of the time she was complaining to me about something and in my attempt to be helpful, I said, "You have four little children (which she knew), and you have a dishwasher." That statement sounds as silly as our first conversation about cucumber skins and burps, but that was forty-some years ago and few young mothers had a dishwasher in those days.

Dottie phoned when she or someone in the family was sick. She *always* knew what needed to be done before she called, but checked in for reassurance. I usually ended my list of suggestions by recommending tomato soup because that's what I like when I'm under the weather. She told me recently, "I hate tomato soup!"

Dottie is an incredible interior decorator. A picture of her home belongs on the cover of *Home and Garden* or some similar magazine. She has a collection of before and after examples of the homes she has decorated. Somehow she works miracles by moving furniture, hanging mirrors and pictures and adding new lamps. Dottie did that for me, too. I had completed my treatments for breast cancer but had not yet finished decorating the new condo we had moved into. I was too tired, weary and needed a vacation. While my husband and I were away, Dottie came to my home and added the final touches to the living room. She left the price tags on everything so what I didn't like or want could be returned. What a wonderful gift that was.

She's been a great sounding board for my own gripes and usually has a different interpretation or slant on events than I do. She's always been there for me. Usually she ends our phone conversations with, "Here's a joke for you before I hang." I've decided to keep Dottie close to my heart for another fifty years or until cucumbers cease to exist.

ELLA

Most of us don't need a psychiatric therapist as much as a friend to be silly with.

—Robert Brault

Judging by the appearance of the tops of our desks or our kitchens, one might conclude that Ella and I are opposites. I can't stand clutter. Everything has to be in its proper place and organized. Ella on the other hand thrives in clutter somehow. But there's one thing we have in common. **We both think the same things are funny**. She makes a comment or an observation and my mind develops a literal picture that sends me into fits of laughing. For example: we were invited to a friend's house for a barbeque. As we pulled into the driveway the friend's rotund father was sitting on the farmer's porch. Ella said, "There's humpty dumpty waiting to greet us." My eyes converted the old man into an oval egg sitting on an imaginary wall and I lost it.

Ella and I were colleagues in a team-taught nursing course: "Nursing care of the Family." I taught the obstetrical clinical component and she the pediatric one. Together, we wrote some chapters in a published nursing textbook. When Ella became pregnant with her first child, she called me at home. "You're familiar with the obstetricians at the hospital. Which one would you recommend for me to go to?" I said I liked Dr. Ford. He's one of the older docs on staff, but he's very respectful of nurses and has excellent clinical skills. Her pregnancy experience and our discussions about it is probably how our friendship began. I offered to coach her and her husband, Dave through labor and delivery. She liked that idea. As it got closer to her due date, I would call her after nine holes on the golf course to make sure she hadn't started labor yet. My clinical days in obstetrics with the students were on Thursdays and Fridays from 7:00 AM to 3:30 PM. I was rounding up the students at 2 PM on a Friday afternoon for a clinical conference when Ella and Dave arrived in the labor and delivery suite. I sent the students home and devoted my time and expertise to Ella's care. Dr Ford came by to check on things.

"Dr. Ford, Ella would like to deliver naturally. Please let us do this our way. We'll call when we see 'fifty cents of caput' (the baby's head)." He backed out of the room saying, "OK." It was uncommon at that time for a mom to call the shots regarding childbirth. Things are different and better today in that regard. Parents are more in charge of their birthing experiences. When the baby's head was in view, I had the staff call Dr. Ford. Ella delivered her baby at 4:30 PM. She and her husband handled labor and delivery like it was a 'piece of cake.' I left reminding Ella that her own knowledge and expertise in pediatrics could now 'kick in.'

Sharing that experience with Ella and Dave was the beginning of a forty-five year friendship. We have been joined at the hip ever since. It would be an understatement to say that Ella and I have had many interesting adventures.

The dean of our college had a death in her family. We decided to go to the wake. Ella drove her car into the city. On the way there we spotted a nice looking Italian restaurant. "That's where we should eat on the way home," she said. So that's what we did. Ella parked in a lot next to the restaurant and although it was a chilly, rainy, November evening, we decided to leave our coats in the car. We enjoyed the pleasant, leisurely ambiance of the place and had delicious Italian food. All of that was spoiled when we discovered Ella's car was gone from the lot. That's when we first noticed the sign on the building next door: "Parking for Norton Liquors Customers Only. All others will be towed at owner's expense." I went into the package store to find out what had happened to the car. The clerk knew what I wanted and without a word, handed me a slip of paper with a telephone number on it. I looked puzzled. "That's where your car is," he said finally. Ella called the number from the restaurant phone and learned the car was several miles away in an impounded lot. We called for a taxi and waited outside the restaurant without our coats. No taxi came. We called for another taxi and this time took turns waiting outside. That taxi didn't come either. "We'll have to try another strategy," I said. I went back into the bakery side of the restaurant to size up the customers, hoping I could find someone in there with a gentle-looking face that might help two damsels in distress. I settled on a man who looked like he was getting ready to leave.

"My friend and I have a problem. We need someone to help us. Our car was towed."

"Was it next door?"

"Yes."

"That bastard! He's done it again. That's why I'm building a parking lot across the street for my customers. If you can wait five minutes, I'll take you to your car."

"Are you the owner, then?"

"Yes, indeed. I'm Peter Bertoncini."

Mr. Bertoncini escorted us to his BMW and drove us to the lot where the car had been towed. As we went, I tried to be grateful and charming by speaking to him in my limited Italian. Ella was amazed by what I was doing but even more amazed by what happened next. The entrance to the fenced-in impound lot was through a trailer manned by a big ape of a guy. Mr. Bertoncini went inside with us and asked the ape what the charge was. "$120.00!" Mr. Bertoncini opened his wallet chock full of paper money and peeled off twelve tens. He then waited outside the trailer until he saw we were safely on our way home.

My husband was shocked. "You got into a car with a man you didn't know? Are you crazy?"

"But he had a nice face."

I sent Mr. Bertoncini a thank you note and about a month later my husband and I went back to his restaurant. We asked for the owner to come to our table so we could thank him again personally.

Ella and I attended a nursing educators' curriculum workshop in Chicago. My cousin lives in that area and invited me out to dinner at a fancy restaurant one evening. Ella had tickets to attend a concert that same night. She let me borrow her red plaid suit which was dressier than the clothes I had brought. My cousin picked me up in his Mercedes with velour, upholstered seats and took me to one of his favorite restaurants. At the entrance he was addressed, "Good evening, Mr. Randall. How are you, Mr. Randall? Will you be seated at your usual table? Will you be using your private phone?"

We ate and chatted and at the end of the meal, my cousin said he'd meet me next to the pool and fountain in the lobby while he went to fetch our coats. Then 'out of the blue' a huge man wearing a tuxedo came by. He picked me up, carried me over to the pool and dropped me in. The water was only about a foot and a half deep, but I landed on my bum and was soaked up to my waist. Then my cousin came along. "Giulia what happened?" Of course he acted all innocent. "What man in a tuxedo? I didn't see anyone like that around." Back at the hotel, I had to explain to Ella why the skirt of her suit was all wet. I couldn't blame her for not believing me. She probably thought I was drunk and fell in the pool. To this day my cousin won't admit he arranged the whole fiasco. But he denies it with a chuckle and a smirk that confirms he's guilty as hell. The next day he asked me to lunch at the Sears Tower. I said, "No thanks, I'm still trying to get my clothes dry." I took the whole suit to the dry cleaners when we got home and fortunately there was no damage to it.

When Ella was very pregnant with her second son, I was taking a graduate level course at a university in another state. It was either a psychology or sociology course entitled "Couples, Marriage and Family." The first assignment was to go to a singles bar to witness coupling behaviors and then write a paper on those observations. The professor had a list of singles' bars we might visit. I was not crazy about the project, but Ella said she'd go with me. We sat at a table rather than at the bar so her gravid body would not be so obvious. Ella really got into the assignment. She elbowed me saying, "Look at that one in red next to the piano. Watch how she operates." Another nudge, "Watch the chick in white at the bar." Still another nudge. "See the guy at the end of the bar? What's he up to?"

"Stop poking me with that elbow. I'm going to be black and blue before the evening is over."

It became clear that that guy at the end of the bar was sizing us up. Where there were two of us, he needed a companion to make his move. He went to the in-house phone and made a call. Then he alternated his attention between the two of us and the door to the bar, obviously waiting for his buddy to arrive.

"Ella, let's get out of here. I don't want to have an encounter with single guys." We got up and went to the cash register at the bar to pay our bill. The guy who had been eyeing us said, "You're not leaving now are you? The fun's just about to begin." Once we were in the car we thought the whole experience was hilarious. We still laugh about that nutty night. I could just imagine what his reaction would have been if I had said, "Get lost buddy. I'm only here to write a paper for college." I did write about the plastic society of a singles' bar. The paper got an A-.

Ella has gone through several phases of "It's time to get beautiful." One effort in that regard led to her getting a set of acrylic nails. Ella's fingers are short and stubby and she's bitten her nails so they are a quarter of an inch below the tops of each finger. As a result, there's a bulge of flesh above each nail. To glue on some artificial nails is tricky because they won't lay flat - they stick up over those bulges. After the application of a set of nails, she was given a special type of super glue to reattach a nail should one fall off. Some did. Dave had to move the refrigerator several times to look for missing nails. One day, on the pediatric unit at the hospital, there was an ugly, gross, yellowish toe nail pinned to the bulletin board. Someone had attached a note above it, "Ella, is this your fingernail?" Ella carried that glue in the pocket of her uniform. It must have leaked because when she got home after a day of clinical, she found that her smock was stuck to her uniform, then to her slip, pantyhose and her underpants. The glue was so strong that she couldn't separate the clothing without ripping them all apart. Another time, she had that glue on her finger and touched her eye. The lids of that eye got stuck together. Dave drove her to the hospital's emergency room to get the lids separated. The beautiful nail program was abandoned. Today Ella's walking around with those same stubby fingers and unadorned nails.

Her next 'body beautiful' effort involved wearing contact lenses instead of eyeglasses. Inserting the lenses onto one's eyeball takes coordination, dexterity and patience. Ella had a problem putting the lenses in place. She was too tense. She called her old buddy from nursing school days who wore contact lenses to have the friend walk her through the procedure. The friend suggested Ella have a glass of wine to relax. Ella had a glass of wine and then another and called the friend back, to start the process over again-with yet another glass of wine for good measure. With a lot of sticking and poking, she finally got the lenses in place. Her husband came home a short time later, and as she descended the staircase, Ella asked, "Do you notice anything different about me?" He said, "Yes, your eyes are swollen and bloodshot and you're drunk." Today Ella wears glasses. I'm glad Ella has given up on all these beauty attempts. She is, to my eyes, perfect and lovely the way she is.

Ella prides herself on her culinary skills. She cooks tasteful and healthy meals. The clothes she buys are often too long. We made a bartering arrangement where I would shorten her sleeves and pant legs and she would supply a meal for my family. The only problem was that she prepared meals that my children or husband would enjoy. They weren't the ones doing the sewing! Nevertheless, the arrangement did spare me from kitchen duty every now and then. I don't claim to be a great cook. I'm not bad, but I'd rather sew, knit or crochet. I do, however, make a mean New England clam chowder that everyone loves – including Ella. She 'borrowed' my recipe, added thyme and called it her own! I objected. She now calls her version the Giulia and Ella clam chowder.

If there is a kitchen, Ella thinks she is in charge of it. She and Dave came to visit us for a week when we were vacationing in Southern California. Expecting additional company, we divided up the chores of menu preparations. I did my cooking, but when I went to serve my creation, I discovered that paprika had been generously sprinkled on top of it. "What did you do to my dish?" I asked.

"I added paprika because it needed color. Don't worry, it won't change the taste."

Ella broke her ankle skiing and had surgery to pin the fractured bones in place. The operation was performed at the hospital where we both did clinical supervision of nursing students. She was put in a cast from her toes to above her knee. Ella requested a room in the pediatric ward so she would be with the nursing staff she knew and worked with. She asked me to stop by to check up on her. The problem with her room assignment was that the accommodations were designed for babies and children – not for a grown woman with an extended leg in a cast. When I arrived, Ella said, "Hurry, I need to go bad." She managed to get herself into an adult wheelchair, but I had a hell-of-a-time trying to maneuver her around corners to get to the bathroom. I kept up a running and chuckling dialog about our being on a pediatric unit as we turned, twisted and bumped into walls. Ella said, "Stop that! Don't say another thing, or I'm not going to make it to the toilet in time."

Ella was diagnosed with breast cancer two years before I was. When she came home from the hospital after a surgical mastectomy, I stayed with her a few hours each day. My job was to reapply a breast binder to keep it snug. Ella can cook – but no one can put on a breast binder better than I can. Who knows what was funny about the circumstances? Somehow we found reasons to laugh. Ella's been cancer-free for over twenty years and was right there for me when I developed breast cancer myself. (See Chapter 10.)

As far as pedagogy goes, we varied our teaching strategies in the classroom. Using a lecture method exclusively did not suit us. It's too boring both for the instructor and the students. But it does take more effort and time to prepare interactive class presentations.

Ella was teaching a class on nurse theorists and nursing theories as part of the course "Introduction to Professional Nursing." She thought it would be particularly memorable if Florence Nightingale herself would come to class to explain her theory of nursing. Guess who was to be Florence? This is what I wore to class: brown oxford tie shoes that belonged to Ella's mother, a long navy blue skirt, a navy blue nurse's cape and a cap Ella made that looked like something the Pillsbury Dough Boy should wear. I prayed nobody would look out any windows as I hurried across the campus in that get-up. I knocked on the door of Ella's classroom at the designated time. A student opened the door and Ella welcomed me with, "Well good morning Miss Nightingale. How nice of you to stop by to meet our students. Would you kindly share with us your theory of nursing care?"

To introduce the flavor of the life and times of Florence Nightingale, I started my presentation by telling the students to look out the window at the Thames River. "See the pollution there. That is the cause of disease. Cleanliness is imperative to prevention and treating infection. By the way, I was born on May 12, 1820." I noticed the students were writing fast and furiously in their notebooks. "Excuse me, but what are you all writing down? Are you planning to send me birthday cards? Close your notebooks and just absorb what I'm explaining about the basis of good nursing care. You won't forget anything, I promise." Ella had the class videotaped. It is amusing and it did capture the intent and objectives of the course.

Trying to get the attention of incoming freshmen students at orientation sessions is difficult. They are tired from staying up all night and they are starting to establish their niche in the scheme of things. As Director of Academic Advising for the university, the critical message I wished to convey to them was "Do not let yourself end up with an F in any course. It is deadly to your cumulative average and will limit your options. If you think you might fail a course, come see me so I can tell you how to avoid a potential problem." To get and hold their attention, I thought to try something crazy. (This was around the time I had had bunion removal surgery and was wearing a duck shoe and using a crab crutch.) When I entered the auditorium, I was wearing a brown, paper, grocery bag over my head. Ella escorted me up front and I held the microphone underneath the bag. I was a sight for sore eyes, to be sure, and the auditorium became very quiet. Adding drama and mystery to my presentation, I asked, "Professor Ella, I need to tell these students something in complete confidence – something I don't want any faculty member to know about. I don't want anyone in administration to know that I am the one who told them what I am about to say. Are the doors shut? Are there any faculty spies present?"

"The coast is clear. You can reveal your secret message," said Ella.

So I took the bag off my head. Some guy at the back of the auditorium yelled out, "Put the bag back." I never used that strategy again. It's one of the bombs Ella likes to remind me off. She did an imitation of me with a bag over her head at my retirement party.

Ella likes to push my buttons. She claims I offer lots of material for her to work with. I tell her to "shut up" quite often. We love each other.

ADELE

Yesterday brought the beginning tomorrow brings the end, and somewhere in the middle we became the best of friends.
—Author Unknown

"Adele, I can't find my crutch."

"You had it with you when you went to the ladies' room. Maybe you left it there. I'll go down the hall and have a look for it."

(Later) "If you could walk all the way back from the ladies' room without that crutch, perhaps you don't need it."

Adele was my secretary at the university when I was director of the advising center and honors programs. She was my right hand and became my dear, dear friend. I had had bunion removal surgery and was wearing a 'duck shoe' and using a crab crutch. Typically, Adele was looking after me when my crutch went missing. She was that way with the students also. Around freshman orientation time, we were stretched to the max with handling student schedules, advising sessions, placement testing, counseling parents, and a million details.

"Is it time for lunch yet? I'm starving."

"You ate your lunch half an hour ago." Adele informed me. "It was a chicken salad sandwich!"

How did I get so lucky as to have such a warm sensitive, caring person by my side during all those challenging years of developing two new academic programs at the university? It was welcome news when I was informed I could hire a secretary full time.

However, I would have to share her with a professor in the math department who was a prolific grants writer. Adele would type up his grant proposals and seminar presentations which neither of us understood. They were all about teaching Calculus through simulated miniature car races. There were about four or five applicants for the position. Adele had worked at the university about sixteen years earlier, before she adopted her son. In that time period, computers had crept into our existence and then became critical to our advising and honors functioning.

In Adele's recollection of my interview with her, she remembers seeing a container for my dental retainer on my desk. Where she wore one also, she says we had a discussion about that topic. At some point I asked what she knew about using computers.

"I'm sorry, but when I stopped working, I was taking dictation and typing with carbon paper. No. I don't know anything about computers," answered Adele.

"Can you learn?"

"Yes, I'd love to. My sister, in the College of Business, is 'up to the minute' on the use of computers and she will help me learn."

Truth be told, I had asked employees who had worked with Adele previously and they couldn't say enough positive things about what a conscientious, committed worker she was. A few of the other applicants had computer experience, but they didn't warm my heart the way Adele did.

Adele always had an even disposition: never up and never down. It's so easy to work with someone like that because you never have to waste mental energy trying to accommodate the other person's moods. I thought Adele was somewhat naïve and I recall only two times when she expressed her view about some of the crazies (both students and faculty) who came through the advising center. She would simply say, "Eeeeeee!"

"I'm wondering if that Laura in the computer lab may have had a sex change. She looks like she's supposed to be a man. Don't you think so?"

I burst out laughing because I didn't think Adele knew about such things and she caught me off guard with that observation.

"I never thought about it," I replied.

I could never look at that Laura again without picturing wide-eyed Adele and her innocent sounding statement about a sex change. Eeeeeee!

She told me about one of the technicians whose job was to set up equipment in a particular lab that the students would need for their assigned experiments each day. On certain times of the year that technician arrived at work forty-five minutes early because she felt the need to remove all the night crawlers that were on the walkway leading up to the building. She picked them up one-by-one and placed them gently on the grass. I suspect they were the same worms she had to move each day. They probably waited all night for her to come and offer such tender loving care. Eeeeeee!

Adele would come in on weekends if I needed help. Her husband, Ted, brought in their son's red flyer wagon and we'd assemble all the advisors' packets, load them into the wagon and deliver them around campus. There is more about Adele and me working, inventing and laughing together in Chapter 6.

Adele saw the good and believed in everyone. If a student came by with a dismal academic record, she would suggest, "Maybe he's working too many hours" or "perhaps she's from a troubled family." By the time I retired, Adele had been promoted to the position of administrative assistant and we were the best of friends staying in touch and getting together as often as possible.

Sadly, Adele called when Ted was diagnosed with lung cancer that had metastasized. He had been admitted to a hospital and then transferred to a large nursing home. He was transported daily to another facility to receive cancer treatments. Ted was not happy.

"Adele, ask Ted if he'd rather be at home. If he says 'yes,' find out if you can arrange for him to be transported for treatments from home. Have the social worker at that nursing home look into it for you. Have the doctor order home care from the Visiting

Nurse Association. You need to do this, Adele, so you'll feel good about yourself at the end. Take a leave of absence."

"But I'm afraid I won't be able to take care of him. I'm scared because I know he's going to die. How will I cope with all that and his sickness?"

"If Ted wants to die at home, you need to make that possible. Adele, you are stronger and more able than you give yourself credit for. I will come and stay with you as much or as often as you want or need me."

Adele got up the courage. At her next visit to Ted, she said, "Giulia suggested I ask if you would rather be at home than here. If that's what you want, we can arrange it."

Ted said, "YES! And God bless Giulia." (Ted didn't want to ask to be at home because he didn't want to be a burden to Adele.)

Everything went according to plan. When I called to see if she wanted me to come by and help. Adele would say, "No, I'm doing OK." Eventually, I would say, "I'm coming one day this week. Which day do you want me to come?" At first, Ted was still able to enjoy and laugh at a good story. He had a great sense of humor and always had a story to tell too. So I told him about a recent golf vacation my husband and I had taken.

We stayed in a nice hotel and were scanning the TV options. Porno movies were available. Like a couple of kids, we studied the list of raunchy titles, selected one, got into our night clothes and clicked the one we had chosen. Nothing happened. We clicked other options. Nothing. My husband called the front desk. The clerk said he'd send up an 'engineer.' So we put our clothes back on and waited. At the knock on the door, we opened it to admit a scruffy looking character in wrinkled work clothes. He went to the TV to check it out and said he'd have to come back to fix the problem. A short time later he returned and did something to the back of the TV. As he passed by me, I nearly gagged. He had a terrible odor: a cross between stale urine and year-old perspiration. He left saying, "Now you can call the front desk and order the channel you want." After he left, I looked at my husband and said, "Oh my God. I'm sick

from the looks and smells of that guy." My husband said, "Me too."
So he called the front desk – "We've decided to watch the ballgame."

When I got to the last line, Ted roared. He wanted to know the
name of the hotel because he planned to send my husband a porno
movie for Christmas. It was to be from the manager of that hotel.
But by Christmas Ted's illness had progressed and sending a porno
movie was the furthest thing from his mind. Adele was a fabulous
care giver. Tiny as she is, she could hold the back of his belt and
help hoist him up a short flight of stairs to the den so he could sit
in his favorite recliner chair. She made him soups, gave appropriate
meds and made him feel comfortable and loved.

I couldn't believe all the friends who came and went each day.
It was like Grand Central Station. And the phone rang all the time.
Ted and Adele meant a lot to so many people: their son, three
grandchildren, a priest, a doctor, fellow members of his Masonic
Lodge, neighbors, a cousin and so many others.

Ted suffered fits of coughing. It was difficult to position and
support him when the coughing started. On Valentine's Day he
experienced another coughing episode. Adele was holding on to
him and Ted died in her arms. I suspect he ruptured a major blood
vessel during that coughing spell and he died suddenly. Ted had
told his son that he wanted to come back as a hawk. I'm not sure
why. However, Adele had called me right after Ted's passing. When
I arrived, the hearse was just leaving. A hawk was circling around
overhead! Adele asked that I present a eulogy at the funeral service. I was pleased and honored to do so. It was so easy to prepare
– the words just flew from my heart to the paper. Among other
things, I had to remark that I didn't know the color of Ted's eyes
because I never got past the twinkle that was always there.

Theirs was a loving, respectful enjoyable relationship. Adele
misses Ted terribly. She now says, "I can look back at a very sad
time in my life knowing that I did all I could do with no regrets,
thanks to my friend Giulia."

She's wrong. She could and would have done it all without me.
Along the way she became a computer whiz.

THERESE

"It takes a long time to grow a friendship"
—John Leonard

I don't think Therese liked me at first. Her husband's best friend had divorced his wife and he subsequently married me. Perhaps she thought of me as the cause of that marriage's breakup. At any rate, my husband had been friends with Therese's husband, Tony, since they were about five or six years old. They are very loyal to each other. When Tony relocated to Southern California we visited the couple every year around Thanksgiving time and usually stayed in a rented condo for three or four weeks. My husband and I played a lot of golf during that time; but we got together with Tony and Therese a couple times a week, at their house, at a restaurant and sometimes at our condo.

Tony is also loyal to his wife Therese; but that's not apparent when you first meet them. There often seems to be a lot of unrest between them. I think much of the angst comes from Tony expecting perfection from everyone. He is high-strung and is particular about the way things are done. Thus, there is occasionally high tension in their home environment.

Visiting their home one day, I was shocked to see their two birds, each in a separate cage, with no feathers on their body except for some on the tops of their heads. "What's wrong with these birds? Do they have a mite infestation or a disease?" "No," replied Tony. "We were advised to take them to a bird psychiatrist for evaluation. He concluded that the birds' environment was making them nervous and causing them to pluck out their feathers." (Of course they couldn't reach the feathers on the tops of their heads.) "We need to take them some place where they'll be adopted into another home."

"Do you mind if I put the covers over their cages? It's difficult for me to look at such 'bare-bolicky' birds. They look obscene." This same tension probably affects Therese sometimes.

On one of our early visits, the university where my husband and Tony graduated from hosted a lobster and clam boil in the desert for alums living in that area of the country. I thought it was quite a treat to be eating clams, lobsters and all the fixings flown in by plane that morning. I said something to that effect to Therese. She replied, "I'd rather be home cleaning." My thought was, "Therese is having a bad day for some reason I don't understand."

So as not to get involved in debating issues with Tony, I would bring my knitting and immerse myself in that activity. Having to count stitches is a great way to stay out of trouble. The problem with listening to Tony is that he inflicts a high level of intensity in his conversation no matter what the subject. It can be wearing. However, Tony is an excellent cook, a talented artist, has a beautiful singing voice and a discriminating taste for high quality clothing, food, etc.

Therese had an accident. She tripped over her dog, fell on the floor and dislocated her shoulder. She was operated on and returned to work when she had recovered. Her job was in a photo lab. Incoming film and outgoing pictures were put in special bags. But someone had put heavy items in the film bag and when Therese went to yank it down from the shelf, the weight of it pulled her arm out of its socket, damaging that same shoulder all over again. More surgery was performed, but the outcome was unsatisfactory. Tony and Therese believe the doctor damaged nerves during surgery because Therese could no longer move her fingers normally. Her fingers wanted to curl down and she couldn't straighten them out. She was given a brace to attach to her wrist that had five metal extensions each with elastic to fasten to the fingers to try to keep them extended. It was ugly looking. Tony and Therese felt that her handicap could be blamed on the surgeon and result in a successful lawsuit. If they were awarded compensation, they believed they might have an easier time of it financially. Tony became very solicitous of Therese, making meals, doing the shopping, laundry and running errands. Therese sat on the kitchen table bench watching her little TV and allowed herself to be waited on for the first time in her life. They couldn't get a lawyer to take on the case. It's very hard to prove medical negligence. Experts (other doctors) have to testify with certainty that this surgeon was totally at fault. Finding a doctor (or two) to make that kind of statement regarding Therese's injury would be just about impossible said the lawyers they met with. The routine of their home life had changed and Therese kept it that way enjoying being on the receiving end of attention even if she wasn't able to bring in the financial compensation they had envisioned.

That was the state of affairs when we next visited. Again, after a meal at their dining room table, I knit away during the conversations. Therese watched me and talked to me about all the knitting she had done in the past. She wanted to start knitting again and wondered if it would be possible with her hand and arm the way they were. I believed it could be done. "Hold the knitting in place with your left hand and work the needle with the right. In the olden days, women wore a belt with slots that had different size holes in it. They would stabilize the left needle by putting it in the best fitting hole and knit with the right hand. They could use their free left hand for carrying things as they walked from one place to another doing errands." Therese tried knitting and that proved to be an excellent exercise for getting her fingers moving better. She caught the bug. She's a knitting addict just like I am. She continues to sit in her spot in the kitchen and has everything she needs on either side of her: every size needle (straights, circulars and double-pointeds), every size crochet hook, the latest knitting magazines and all the catalogs from yarn distributors. We talk knitting non-stop when we're together and over the phone when I'm at home. Therese doesn't drive or get out much because she doesn't have good balance. But when I come to town, we hit the craft stores in her area. We gossip and commiserate about life.

Out of the blue one day she said, "I never had any brothers or sisters, but you're the one I would have loved to have had as a sister." We have called each other 'Sis' ever since. It did take time to build that friendship and I'm honored to have it.

Incidentally, Tony has thanked me many times for "What you did for my wife. You are her angel."

PENNY

A friend knows the song in my heart and sings it to me when my memory fails.
—Donna Roberts

Penny is my newest friend-sister. We've known each other about four years but it feels as though we've been close friends since childhood. She's smart, sensitive, serious and beautiful. She is more patient with people than anyone I have ever known. She is a teaching coach for high school students with Asperger's.

Here's what I love about Penny:
- She remembers the details of everything I tell her and brings them back into the picture when they're relevant.
- She knows what I'm thinking and what's in my heart and has the perfect words to help me express myself.
- She acts the devils' advocate when I'm trying to make a decision or trying to clarify my thoughts.

We like to walk together in nice weather and we exercise our jaws as much as our legs. I love being with Penny. I come home feeling like I've had a therapeutic therapy session.

CHAPTER 9

THE RED BOX

There's a red container on my front stairs that looks like a specimen box one would see outside a doctor's office – A box that holds urine and blood samples until a lab comes by for pickup. Fortunately, no one has left any kinds of bodily fluids there (yet). Instead, it is place for knitters to put their mistakes. I call it the "knitting orphans'" box.

Knitting is my passion and has been fulfilling a niche in my retirement years. My home has two finished rooms in the walk-out basement. The larger one is where the hand knitting takes place while the smaller room is for sewing, steaming and machine knitting. If I were to tell you there are over a thousand skeins and cones of yarn in the knitting room, you would probably doubt it. But there is also a large cedar closet off the hallway that stores all the wool yarn. For a yarn and knitting addict such as me, this is a heavenly environment. There's a wall mounted TV and a stereo system there, also.

I live in a neighborhood where there are lots of retired grand-parents who are yearning to begin knitting children's' things. So I started a club. Pay $50 per year, and come on Thursdays to open house knitting. In between times, if you make a mistake, leave it in the box (which I check every day) and it'll be fixed for you. I encourage the knitters to try fixing mistakes themselves and if they should make things even messier, I can always take care of it. Lost a stitch 20 rows ago? No problem, I'll latch it up for you. There's no need to rip it out.

Right now I have approximately 35 active knitters on the books that are at all levels of expertise. They all think I'm super smart and am very generous with the time I devote to them. They don't quite grasp that the rewards are practically all mine. When a knitter finishes something that they didn't think they could ever do, and loves the way it looks and fits, it makes my little heart strings flutter. Gradually they learn to fix their own mistakes and start looking for something more challenging. "Do you think I could do cables now?" Of course, "Let's do it!"

Two of my knitters started sweaters a few years ago before they met me. We call them the 5 or 6 year sweaters. Unfortunately both sweaters are very, very large. I tell them their sweaters are only ten stitches away from being tents. That doesn't deter them. They're bound to finish them, wear them with several people inside and walk their dogs. The encouraging thing is that they are both talking about their next project and how much better that will be.

How did the obsession with knitting and yarn begin? I was about six and spent some time at my grandmother's house when my parents were working. My aunt and her husband lived in the family homestead also. I thought my aunt was really cool. She was younger than my mother, set her hair in pin curls and went to the movies with two other couples on a Saturday night. To my eyes she had an enviable lifestyle. AND she knitted! She had a square knitting basket sitting on the floor next to a comfortable chair. The yarn and needles sticking out of it intrigued me so much. What did she have going on in that basket? I suspect that with my fascination with her projects, she decided to satisfy my curiosity and teach me to knit. She gave me some leftover thin blue yarn, put the stitches on a needle and with her help I proceeded to make a pair of mittens. They were a little too thin to be practical, but I was addicted. My instant success with knitting pleased my mother. She contributed to my new hobby by making my first knitting bag. It was a round Quaker Oats box which she covered with wallpaper. She put a hole in the top for the yarn to come through and put rope handles on the sides. That bag and I were inseparable. Even today I can feel the pride I had when walking down the street carrying my special knitting bag.

Other people then wanted to contribute to my needling skills. The little Portuguese woman in the first floor level of our tenement taught me to crochet. I made a round mat with rug yarn. It was pretty and colorful, but not really safe as a floor mat. Without a backing it would slip and slide all over the place.

Next my grandmother wanted to get into the act. She took a square piece of cotton cloth, gave me a fine hook and thin crochet thread and taught me to crochet lace around that piece of fabric.

Long after I needed a babysitter, my mother hired a woman from an adjacent town to stay with my sisters and me one evening and teach me to tat. Tatting is a very fine lace made with a shuttle or needle. It is beautiful but very tedious to make. I do not tat very often.

I knitted or crocheted through high school and college. During our psychiatric nursing rotation we had to experience and participate in simulated "group therapy." At one of the sessions, the therapist asked, "How does the group feel about Giulia's knitting during our meetings?" Everyone spoke out, some saying, "It doesn't bother me," or "Whatever," or, "She participates as much as the rest of us." Others went on about my knitting possibly preventing me from participating fully. After a round of all that blah, blah, blah, the psychiatrist then asked, "Giulia, how do you feel about what's been said?" I said it didn't matter what other people thought, I had Christmas presents to make and I was not going to stop knitting. Of course, he then asked the group what they thought of my answer and the talking went round and round some more while I continued to knit.

There was a time when I couldn't knit. That was when my mother passed away. She was genuinely interested in my needlework projects. When I was about ten, I remember her saying things like, "Giulia, show Aunt Irene the purse you crocheted this week" or "How did you know how to knit with four needles?" Because neither of my sisters showed any inclination toward needlework, I felt that I was earning some unique motherly love because of what I could do with those needles. She was proud of my work and me. She even bought me a subscription to *McCall's Needlework Magazine*. I felt accomplished and mature and I have all those periodicals still. You could say my mother and I had a strong emotional attachment to each other through needlework. When she died I lost my anchor, my threads became frayed and then broke. For almost a year I was unable to comfort myself with knitting or any kind of needlework, for that matter. It pleases me, however, to remember that I was able to help her with her sewing now and then. Changing the threads in an overlock machine is quite complicated. I often stopped by her house on my way home from work to get her overlock rethreaded. I made more of her drapes, curtains and pillows than you could shake a stick at. In the end, after she passed away, I went through her sewing box and finished off every single thing she had started.

I would dearly love it if everyone could come to know the comfort, relaxation and pride that knitting can provide. I share what I know with others and by doing so I am also sharing some of my mother, my aunt and my grandmother. I have only been burned (or stabbed) once in helping others through knitting. It is an ugly story.

One knitter was going through a difficult period. She was getting divorced from her handicapped husband, her daughter was getting married and she wanted to lose 20 pounds and make her own mother of the bride dress. Further, she wanted to sell or rent her home and then move into a subsidized apartment. First, I tried to help her organize her thoughts regarding the divorce in preparation for discussions with a lawyer. With all that was going on I convinced her to forget making a dress. (What she had done didn't look that great anyway.) "Order something from a catalog and make it easier on yourself," I suggested. This she did and made several visits to my home to try on various dresses for my approval. After settling on one, she asked me to knit a shawl to go with it. I assumed she would pay me, but she never did. In fact, after the wedding she asked me to make it longer.

Then came the task of packing. She was so disorganized. It was in the heat of summer that I was at her home on many days to help her – bringing lunch to boot. It never occurred to me that I was falling into the trap of a very needy person. Women need to help women is what I believe, so I continued. "Let's start in this room, go counter clock-wise and put each item in one of three piles: things to be packed for moving to the new apartment, things to be put in storage and things to be put in the garage for a future yard sale." I wrapped and packed and wrapped and packed. She asked me to be there on moving day. At the new place, I unpacked, laid out the carpets, got her bedroom furniture situated and made up the bed. For the moving men I bought (and paid for), subs, pizzas and sodas.

She didn't come to knitting after that. One of her previous neighbors said she'd had surgery on her hand and couldn't knit. Months later, at a regularly scheduled knitting session, she showed up. "You remember that coat I started knitting? Will you finish it because I can't knit anymore because of problems with my thumb." I suggested that perhaps she could try a different style of knitting to avoid the thumb problem, like holding the needles differently. "No, I don't want to." I said to leave it in the corner and I would have a look at it when I got a chance. Next, she said, "By the way, that table I gave you I would like to have back."

"You didn't give me a table."

"Yes I did. It was in the living room. You liked it, so I took the cover off and gave it to you."

After the knitters left that afternoon, I sent dear Alice an e-mail.

"Alice, it disturbs me that you think you gave me a table. You didn't. Here is a list of the things you did give me because you said you were putting them aside for a yard sale.

- green tablecloth
- black fan
- mattress pad cover
- purple lamp
- tiny footstool."

Within ten minutes of pushing the 'send' button, Alice called. "Did you get the e-mail I sent you?" I asked. "No, what did it say?" (Of course she got it!) I repeated what I had written in the e-mail.

"I know I gave you that table. I remember things like that very clearly."

"Well come over and have a look around."

"You probably gave it to someone else."

"Alice, if I really liked your table, why would I give it to someone else? Furthermore, how would I be able to take home your table? I don't have a truck."

"Didn't you wonder why I haven't been to knitting all this time? It's because I also know you stole some of my figurines."

"Alice, what are you saying? I can't believe you're accusing me of stealing from you."

Then she struck the final blow. "With all your talents and degrees, you think you're better than everyone else."

"That's it," I said. "I won't listen to another word of this non-sense." I hung up.

The next day I mailed off a package, return receipt, with her unfinished knitting. I put a note inside saying, "I am shocked that you would accuse me of stealing. Perhaps your missing items will turn up or you will remember to whom you gave them. In the meantime, I want nothing to do with you." The signed receipt came back.

That was the end of all that unpleasantness – or so I thought.

Perhaps it was almost a year or so later, in the month of November. My daughter was checking my mail while I was vacationing in California. She came across a disturbing piece of mail—a large envelope with no return address. In it was the "I want nothing to do with you" note I had sent Alice, along with a crazy, schizophrenic poem that goes on and on about all the things she can't find. Also, there was a glossy picture of a bureau. On the picture were stickers of the Three Wise Men. Finally, there was a weird Christmas card – stick figures of a crèche scene and it was signed 'Alice.'

I circulated a copy of this material to several people who had known about her original accusations. All thought this seemed scary – that she is sick, but she could be dangerous to me, to herself or to others. Part of me thought she was crying for help. But it would have to be someone else that needed to know about her and what to do for her. Upon my return from California just before Christmas, my husband and I went to the local police department. Half way through my story, Officer Bob says, "I know Alice. I will reach out to her and I will get back to you." He did not say, "Alice is known to us" or "We know about Alice." The '*I* know Alice' peeked my curiosity. A little searching on the internet revealed that Alice had moved yet again and she now lived in a condominium two doors away from Officer Bob.

After the holidays I began calling Officer Bob to see if he had followed through on his promise. I waited one week between each phone call leaving messages for him to get back to me. I was careful not to tamper with his ego. Finally, the third message I left was to suggest that perhaps I should write up the details of my complaint. I innocently inquired to whom I might mail all this information. That's when he did call back! He said he'd been away training, preparing for deployment to Afghanistan. (Don't other officers back him up while he is away?) He promised to get in touch with Alice to explain that what she did was harassment and should she contact me again, she could be cited for a criminal offense. No sooner had I hung up the phone when it rang again. It was Officer Bob. He said, "Alice?" "No, it's me. You called the wrong number."

Later in the day he did call back. He said Alice had come into the station with a lawyer. He said her feelings were hurt. He also said he doesn't live near Alice anymore. He had moved.

This one person figuratively stabbed me with her needles. Did I learn anything from all that. No. On any given Thursday, I look at all my knitters happily clicking their needles, discussing recipes, restaurants, doctors, good books, the latest on TV serials, how to get out stains and just about any other topic under the sun. They are relaxed and happy here and it pleases me that I make this happen. So I will continue to help wherever or whenever I see the need and trust I am never treated like that ever again.

I would be remiss were I to end this subject of knitting with an unpleasant narrative, for there are too many wonderful stories to tell. Here is one: My step-granddaughter was selling Girl Scout cookies. That gave me an idea of something I could make to enter a knitting contest – A Brownie in a Box. My Brownie was a 10 inch knit doll. She had a beanie, braided hair, a little badge sash and all the correct insignia in place. I placed her in a box decorated with Brownie Scout colors (blue and brown. She had her own mattress, pillow and afghan. I sent in a picture of Brownie and learned that I would be a finalist. Therefore, I had to send the actual doll in for final judging. I took her to the local UPS office and felt sad to see her go. As she was evolving, and her twinkling eyes and smiling mouth appeared, she began to have a personality and seem real. But off she went for inspection. Then I learned that she had been put on the wrong truck. True to Girl Scout self-sufficiency she got herself where she needed to go. She won me $500 and a Brownie's grandmother later bought her for $75. (See Appendix C.)

During a recent knitting class, one of the students stood up and said she wanted to read a poem she had written. Here it is:

Ode to Giulia

Knit and purl,
What a girl!
Purl and knit,
She does not sit.
She picks up stitches
And fixes our glitches.

She sews with a skill,
For which others would kill.
Keeping dolls in style
All the while.
Her tale she does spin,
Of being an Irish twin.

Needles and hooks,
Tons of books.
Giulia's got it all,
So give her a call.
Become a knit-wit.
Come sit and knit.

Thank you for everything - Katherine

I knit everywhere; waiting in line or sitting in traffic, and even on the golf course. If I have to wait my turn to tee off, I sit in the golf cart and knit. I never get frustrated if the course of play is slow. At night, in the car, when my husband is driving, I put a small version of a miner's lamp on my forehead and knit away. I even knit in the bathtub. What could be more relaxing and soothing than soaking in a hot tub and feeling the yarn going through one's hands? I do not recommend doing it with 100% wool, but acrylics are fine even when they get wet.

CHAPTER 10

MY LIFE'S BLIPS

There is no question in my mind but what I have lived a charmed life. Ninety percent of the time things have gone my way. I have only taken on battles when I knew I was right and knew I could win. In spite of that, some trials and tribulations did come my way. Using computer lingo, I call them 'blips.'

Prejudice Against Me for Being Female

One holiday in April, there was a men's tournament at a local golf course where I was a member. Unfortunately, that club had a rule that women could not play on Saturdays, Sundays or holidays before noontime. (Unbelievable, but true!) At the last minute, a man dropped out of his foursome and I was asked to replace him. I agreed because the slot had already been registered and paid for. When I stepped up to the first tee, all hell broke loose. The president of the club came up to me in his golf cart saying, "You can't play – it's against the policy of this club." I hit a terrible tee shot. He followed me up to my ball and kept saying, "You have to leave." I am not the world's worst golfer, but I couldn't stand the harassment and couldn't hit the ball, so I left. I was ticked. I agreed to play as a favor to the three men who were without a forth. That rejection was a difficult and bitter pill for me to swallow.

Shortly after that incident, there was a letter to the editor in the local newspaper written by a well-respected female community activist. She was complaining about being denied entrance to the grillroom at a private club. She had been invited by a member to lunch there. Apparently, that member didn't realize women were not permitted to eat in that particular room. The both of them were turned away.

A few nights later there was another letter to the editor written by a doctor's wife defending the 'men only' policy. She stated that doctors need a place to meet where they can share the latest in medical technology; a place where lawyers can meet to discuss the fine points of the law. (Did she not know that there are female doctors and lawyers? Where are female professionals supposed to share and discuss pertinent subjects?)

That point of view really got to me. I got into the fray and wrote my own letter. I stated my position and ended with, "Why should the presence or absence of a penis dictate where one can eat or when one can play golf?" After it appeared in the paper, I received pats on the back and 'right on' everywhere I went.

I told lots of people I should like to get a headband like the one Steve Martin, the comedian, used to wear. It looked like he had an arrow going through his head. I envisioned wearing something similar with an artificial penis sticking out the top. Then, I could approach the first tee or a private men's grill room and announce, "Here I am. I have a penis, so now I can play/eat here." I shared that idea with lots of people. It was good for a few laughs; but I never actually acted on that thought. The nursing laboratory at the university had dummies with changeable parts that allowed students to practice their clinical skills. A professor took one of the dummies to her classroom for teaching purposes. When she got back to the laboratory, the dummy's penis was missing. Naturally, there were comments that suggested, "DaMaglia has it so she can play golf on Saturdays, Sundays and holidays." The penis, it turned out, had fallen off the dummy in the elevator. Fortunately, no one had taken a ride until the penis was found. While there was humor in all of this, I remain quite bitter that there are still people who place so much value on a penis.

THE SKY IS FALLING

All I intended to do that day was deposit my usual, weekly check into my bank account at a free-standing ATM near my home and then hurry back to the university to be interviewed for a position I dearly wanted. It was a windy day. As I stood in front of the machine, there was a crash that sounded like an explosion. It startled me out of my skin and when I looked behind me I saw what had happened. The ceiling, including the large, rectangular, metal box that housed the fluorescent lamps had crashed down and was smashed all over the floor. The cable wires were dangling. I was literally shaking; my legs were like rubber. Next door was a boutique where I went to sit and calm down and explain to the employees what that loud crash was that they had heard. The owner of the property arrived and hustled to clean up the ATM so that it could be available for use by the next customer. He didn't even ask how I was. Later, a lawyer told me that I should have called 911 and been examined in the emergency room of a hospital. At that time, all I could think about was that I needed to pull myself together and get back to the university for that interview. So that's what I did. That evening was when I discovered the bruises on my bum. That rectangular lighting fixture must have hit me on its way to the floor. The fact that no one seemed to care about what had happened to me was the reason I decided to consult a lawyer. I was mad. Because I had not gone to the hospital when it happened, the lawyer said I needed to see a doctor that he recommended. He made two appointments for me. That doctor I would classify as a quack. Mostly we talked about the problems he was having with his daughter and his marriage. Never the less, those two visits satisfied the requirements for a successful lawsuit against the bank. I received five thousand dollars and bought a fur coat. To this day I startle much too easily. Any loud noise shakes my nervous system to the core. The check I was depositing that day was not so enormous that it should have caused the sky to fall. It must have been the wind and certainly lousy construction.

DIVORCE

I believe anyone who says they have had an amicable divorce is lying either to fool themselves or their kids. How can 'I don't love you, I don't like you or I can't stand you' ever lead to a friendly, permanent dissolution of a marriage?

As a freshman in college, I was swept off my feet by a senior guy named Charles. He was fun loving, a great dancer, handy with tools, skilled in industrial arts and had a car. He had lost his father six months earlier and was looking for someone to love to fill the void. Me – a lowly freshman being dated by a senior? After he graduated, we got together many weekends and corresponded in-between times. He had given me his fraternity pin and during my junior year an engagement ring and a cedar hope chest. He dearly wished I would leave school to get married. (Married students are not allowed in the nursing program I attended.) Earning my degree, becoming a nurse and fulfilling my obligations regarding my roles in student government were too important to me to consider dropping out of school. I postponed setting a date for marriage and engaging in serious intimacy. (The birth control pill was not readily available at that time.) My graduation was the beginning of December and our wedding was planned for Christmas time. I admit I had had occasional doubts about whether I had given myself an opportunity to 'explore the field,' but I had kept him on the hook for so long, I didn't have the guts to postpone or call the relationship off. Besides, everyone in my family thought he was super. He was having a new house built for us. I simply let the momentum carry me along, sewed my own wedding gown and finally had a lovely, low-cost wedding with a reception in the church hall. We were supposed to go on a skiing vacation for our honeymoon, but I came down with the flu and didn't feel like traveling very far. Also, I wanted to be back home for Christmas.

The years after were like being on a roller coaster – work, finishing the upstairs and adding on an addition to our home, having two children and installing a pool with an attached cabana. Next, we bought a house with an attached lot, sold the house as well as the home we built on the empty lot. With the profits from selling those two houses, plus our original home, we had another unfinished house built in a lovely seaside community. By this time, I had run out of energy and patience with all the painting, shingling, finish work and nerve wracking real estate transactions that were involved. This was all in addition to the full-time teaching and parental responsibilities I had. Then I took on another part-time job to pay for professional landscaping of our newest home. At night and on weekends, I made drapes, stenciled the bathroom walls, etc. When it seemed like we were finally in a steady state, I came to realized that I was quite unhappy. My husband, a teacher, had 'pie-in-the-sky' ideas of becoming rich. "Let's start a chowder and clam-cake business for the summers," he suggested.

"I don't want to spend my summers cooking and serving food to people."

Next he wanted to buy a large boat, set traps and make money catching and selling lobsters. I didn't want to use my earnings for that.

"Let's get a piece of property at a vacation spot and build a house there." I went along with that plan until a man walking his dog fell through the basement covering, and fractured his leg. I lost a lot of sleep worrying that we could be sued. Finally I said, "Sell the property as is and we'll split the proceeds. I've had enough."

The final 'bright idea' was that five other couples had a plan to buy a time-share condominium somewhere down south. I refused to sign on the dotted line. "You're the only one who's holding up the deal." "Look, I'm not putting up my hard-earned money to get involved in a venture with twenty other people. Count me out." He was furious.

Our approach to the discipline of the children was 180 degrees apart. For example, I couldn't fathom why our son needed a car when the school bus went right by the end of the driveway. My husband managed to buy a car for him, but then I was 'hit up' for mufflers, gas, etc. When they did something wrong, he would tell them, "OK, but don't tell your mother." He would take on a disciplinary role only when I was totally exasperated. Always the 'good guy,' I would always end up on the short end of the stick. Over time I became annoyed with everything he did – if he cleared his throat, it grated on my nerves. I was in a rut. Some of the lyrics from Carole King's 'It's Too Late' resonated with me: "Something inside has died and I can't hide, And I just can't fake it."

Gradually, my husband and I developed an 'in house' separation. He slept in one bedroom and I in another. Then I began to stay with my sister some nights, friends other nights, slept on the couch of our home sometimes and stayed in my father's hospital room when he was terminally ill. I floated around like a 'man without a country.'

My unhappiness must have been obvious to others before I confronted it myself. A very nice man in our bowling league asked if I might accompany him on a week's business trip to Germany. He was a computer engineer who designed bar codes for credit cards. Gradually, I realized that respectable men were flirting with me or making suggestive remarks. I must have been giving off "I'm available" vibes.

I looked at my life. I had three kids instead of two. Even his mother at a later time said, "I understand more than you realize. My son will always be a boy." We had grown (?) in different directions and were miles apart.

Eventually, I met someone whose company I enjoyed. He was a university colleague. We played golf together a few times which I convinced myself was innocent enough. One day we went for lunch after golf and he asked, "I think we have something special going on here – do you?" "Yes," I blurted out. I confess: I then engaged in an affair with this man and knew I must therefore begin divorce proceedings. My daughter was at the end of her high school years. So as not to uproot her, I agreed to let my 'ex' live in the home rent-free for a couple of years. (I had paid off the mortgage.) Letting him live there was a big mistake. He didn't take care of the property. He had it looking like a dump. I was paying the bills for our children's education and he was 'running a tab.' I allowed these things to happen because I felt guilty – I was the one who had broken up the marriage. When it came time to put the house on the market, it sold for half of what it had been worth at the time of the divorce. My generosity had cost me dearly. Fortunately, I had records of everything I had spent on the children and the court ordered him to pay half.

Divorce is a stressful, difficult and painful ordeal to go through. But staying in a relationship that brings unhappiness is even worse. Some time later, after the divorce was final, I brought my new beau to my mother's house so she could meet him. She commented, "I didn't realize how unhappy you were until I see how happy you are now." Years later, I married that man and am living 'happily ever after.'

CANCER

As a nursing student, I had had my first scare about having breast cancer. (See Chapter 4.) After that experience there were several other lumps that turned out be benign tumors or cysts. Once I was scheduled for excision of yet another suspicious lump at a major city hospital. This one was very painful especially when I rolled onto my stomach at night. My husband had to administer final exams that day. He dropped me and my mother off at a street corner where the hospital was located and said he would return to that same spot at a specific time to pick us back up. I went through the pre-op routine and was in my jonnie waiting to be called for surgery. The surgeon came out. "Before we go into the operating room, come into this examining cubicle and let me see if we can aspirate anything from that lump." He inserted a needle attached to a large syringe and out came about thirty cc's of fluid that looked like Coca-Cola. I had instant relief and the lump was gone. Surgery was not necessary this time. "Mom, I don't need surgery and we have two and a half hours before my husband comes back to get us. What should we do?" "Go shopping of course." When my husband came back for us, we were standing on the street corner loaded down with shopping bags.

There were several similar occurrences over the course of many years. Then something different happened. I had my regular mammogram. It was repeated because there was some change from the previous one. Then I was taken into another room for an ultrasound that was done by the radiologist himself. He asked, "When are you scheduled to see Dr. Blake?" "I'm going there from here." "Great, I'll have a chat with him before you get there."

At Dr. Blake's office: "You have everyone worried. That lump needs to be biopsied. Where you've had so many of these episodes before, it is unlikely this one will be anything serious." I was scheduled for that biopsy and two days later Dr. Blake called. "I'm shocked and chagrinned to have to tell you that the biopsy revealed you have cancer. I want you, your husband and a girlfriend to come in now to talk with me. I'll wait until you arrive." We picked up Ella, my girlfriend, and off we went. Where Ella had had breast cancer two years previously, she knew to bring a notebook in which to jot down answers to all the questions she and my husband had. I was much too numb and stunned to say or ask anything. My reaction was this: "If I have cancer cells in me, then get them out of my body immediately before they spread – to heck with the wedding I'm supposed to go to in California next week." "No. You go to that wedding and have a drink on me," said Dr. Blake. "I'll take care of you as soon as you get back."

When I returned, I threw myself into Dr. Blake's arms and said, "Get it all." I was injected with a radioactive solution to highlight which nodes in my armpit were the 'sentinel' ones. Three of them were removed during surgery to see if cancer cells had escaped the original site in the breast. The sentinel nodes and a sizeable portion of my breast tissue was removed. The nodes were negative for cancer. With that finding, it was determined that I needed thirty-three doses of radiation to the breast. Dr. Blake said he didn't see the necessity for chemo.

After the wounds healed, I started radiation. I was dismayed about the radiation routine I encountered. After signing in at the reception desk, I went to a small locker room with old metal lockers and linen dust over everything. Then after donning a jonnie, I sat in a large waiting area with lots of very sick people and a TV blaring nonsense. They were forty-five minutes late calling me in and I was escorted to the radiation room by two males who were doctor 'wanna-be' types wearing white coats. I was uncomfortable exposing my breasts to these two men who were unconcerned about and oblivious to my feelings and fears. My second treatment, handled the same way, occurred on Friday and I informed the staff that I would be back on Monday morning, but would have no more treatments until I met with the radiation oncologist physician. She was there when I came back on Monday. I told her I couldn't continue to come to her facility for radiation anymore, because I was receiving insensitive and impersonal care. I explained, "I took excellent care of my patients for many years. I provided for their comfort in every way possible. Now I want back the same kind of care I gave to others."

"You are the patient. Your needs come first. What do you want us to do?"

"Here's what I want:

- To put my jonnie on in an examination room and to wait there. The locker room is small and depressing. I'll wait here, not in the general waiting area. If I'm supposed to feel positive about my diagnosis of cancer and my own prognosis, that surely can't happen if I'm surrounded by people who look to be at death's door. At a time like this, I have to be concerned about me and what will give me positive thoughts.

- To be escorted to the radiation room by women – not those two brutes I had last week.
- To wear a sweater over my jonnie while I walk the corridor to the radiation room. It only takes two seconds to remove the sweater once I'm there. That won't put anyone behind schedule.
- To be taken within fifteen minutes of my scheduled appointment. This is not a department where unexpected emergencies arise that will cause delay. It is unacceptable to me to be made to wait."

She listened, she understood and she arranged for all my requests to be honored. Thereafter I was taken for radiation within five minutes of my arrival. Sometimes I was already on my way home at the time of appointment. My surgeon was informed of these details. He was unhappy. "I'm embarrassed to think of all the nice ladies I am sending over there to be subjected to that kind of experience." He called in the nurse manager and told her to arrange a team meeting so all this could be addressed.

What amazed me was how many people wanted to help. People I hardly knew came 'out of the woodwork' to ask what they could do. For example, there was a man next door who pretty much kept to himself. He called and asked, "What day of the week would you like me to drive you in to the hospital for your treatments?" (The hospital was fifty miles each way.) We agreed on Wednesdays and there he'd be in the driveway at 8 A.M. sharp every Wednesday. Another neighbor down the street, my former secretary, friends, my children and my husband all took turns transporting me. We'd stop for coffee on the way home. It could almost have been pleasant if it weren't so tiring. I went for those treatments thirty-three times but never once did my sister Pam go with me or even send a get-well card. That hurt more than anything.

The treatment of breast cancer at that facility involved a team approach. Each patient is seen by the surgeon, oncologist, the radiation oncologist, a social worker and a counselor. I didn't feel like going those fifty miles round trip to meet with a counselor, so I opted to meet with a psychiatric nurse practitioner whose practice was nearer to my home. "I'll go through the motions just to satisfy the team's requirement," I thought. "She'll probably pat me on the back and tell me I'm doing a great job coping with all that cancer business." That is not what happened. Five minutes into my first session I was 'spilling my guts.' She zeroed in on one particular topic that was upsetting to me.

That issue had to do with my sister, Pam. I gave her all the details as I knew them. (See Chapter 2.) "Pam has a birthday next month. What should I do about that?"

"Go to the Hallmark store and read all the sister birthday cards. If there is one that expresses a message you think is accurate, then send it. If not, send nothing. This is no time for false sentiments." There was no appropriate card and I was happy she gave me some concrete suggestions and a basis to feel all right with my feelings.

Secondly, she pointed out that I am and probably always have been a fighter. "From all you've told me, your mother encouraged you to be that way. That fighting spirit has served you very well throughout your professional working years. Give those skills back to your mother. You don't need them anymore. Also, you will encounter few people who approach a task at the same level of perfection you do. You should learn to expect less from others." That advice is easier said than done, but I have changed and even let myself be sloppy now and then. I tell my knitting students, "Look, we're not going for perfection here!"

Early May, eleven years out from that cancer diagnosis, I decided to throw a party for girl friends to celebrate spring (although it was pouring rain), happiness and good fortune. I used my knitting funds to pay for the event. My friend Josh said, "If you're throwing a party for friends, then I have to be there."

"But I'm only inviting gals."

"All the more reason for me to be there!"

So I invited him and his wife with the understanding that he, Josh would lead the bunny hop. Sixty people came to the breakfast buffet held at the country club where I now live. I made different crocheted/knitted flower corsages for each guest. My knitting students and others presented a fashion show wearing their knitted fashions. At the appropriate time in the program I called upon Josh to come forward. I donned him in a white coat I borrowed from the meat market and pinned a knitted pink carnation on his lapel. We danced around to the tune of "A White Sports Coat and a Pink Carnation" and then I passed him off to another guest. After that he led the bunny hop which segued into the 'chicken,' etc. (See Appendix B for the entire program and the song lyrics we sang.) One guest was dancing away and said as she passed, "I can't believe I'm doing this so early in the day and without anything to drink!"

Before closing, I shared my feelings, "Having cancer turned out to be a growing experience. I learned what and who matters to me and what and who does not. Each of you touches my heartstrings in a special and happy way. You've been there for me when I needed you. Remember, I will be there for you, too." The party ended with everyone getting into a big circle and singing "May You Always," which was recorded by the McGuire Sisters in 1958. There wasn't a dry eye in the house. It was a wonderful celebration.

HIP BLIP

I never had to 'run for my supper.' One doesn't have to watch many National Geographic documentaries to realize that in some undeveloped countries and in cave man times you had to run or starve. When the food larders were getting low, it was time to target a meaty-looking wild animal and chase it until it fell down exhausted. Then the hunters went in for the kill and enjoyed good eating for many days later. How could men run so much and so far and not fall down with exhaustion like their prey? A 'runners' high' no doubt prevented them from feeling fatigue, shin splints, blisters, etc. With extreme physical exertion, the human body releases endorphins that travel to the pleasure centers of the brain and makes one unaware of pain/discomfort.

I have enjoyed the sensation of the 'runner's high.' I began running around age thirty-five, going five to eight miles each day in good weather. Occasionally, time permitting; I could manage up to fifteen miles in a single outing. Some marathoners describe the 'high' as euphoric. Some have even likened it to an orgasm. My running never produced those sensations, but two things did happen to me. First, I would go into a state of oblivion, getting home with no memory of the last few miles. It was a peaceful feeling. But my brain was busy none-the-less. If I were composing a memo, writing a thesis or a book and suffered 'writer's block,' before my run, the missing sentences or thoughts would pour out of my pencil after an episode of 'runner's high.' Running also helped me escape from the irritations at home. With all these benefits, I ran all over town and along the beaches every chance I could.

A neighbor cautioned me, "All that running isn't good for you. You'll have hip problems when you get older." He was prophetic. The pain was in my groin. I was surprised when the orthopedic doctor explained that this symptom was typical of a hip problem. An x-ray confirmed that my hip (the ball and socket joint) had deteriorated. This doctor is not one to push surgery. He gave me a shot of cortisone and sent me for physical therapy to tone up the muscles supporting that joint. I may have gotten some relief but if I did, it did not last long. My husband and I were visiting friends in

Florida when the pain kept me up all night. Sometimes when the pain struck, I felt like I would fall over if I weren't holding onto something.

I couldn't get back to the doctor fast enough. He said it looked like I was a candidate for a hip replacement. "You'll know when it's time."

"Are you kidding? It was time several weeks ago."

"As soon as you have all the pre-op paper work done, we'll schedule it."

"No. Call and put me on the schedule now. I'll be back this afternoon with all the necessary papers from my general practitioner including all the required lab work. I'm desperate." I had the surgery and the pain was gone. (Of course the pain meds helped!) I felt like I could get up and about immediately, but having lost a lot of blood forced me to stay in bed, be transfused and wait until my lab values were back to normal.

The day after I returned home, my daughter came by to help me. I was dressed up and came out of the bedroom walking with one crutch. She started crying. "What's wrong?" I asked.

"I can't believe you. My friend had some kind of hip surgery six weeks ago and she is still in a wheelchair. I didn't expect you'd be walking around already." At my check up a few weeks later, the surgeon acted as if I were his model patient. "Walk, walk, and walk," he said. So I did. I felt fabulous — so fabulous that I tended to forget I had even had that operation.

One Thursday after knitting classes, I decided I needed to vacuum the floor of the sewing room which my son was finishing for me. I didn't want the sawdust to get tracked around the house. Honestly, I forgot about my hip and any limitations. I know now that bending down and twisting is a maneuver that my new hip could not handle. Out popped my hip. I fainted and fell on the floor with my head only one inch away from a large mirror that was resting on the wall waiting to be installed. I laid there in agony. The least little movement sent my muscles into painful spasms. My husband finally came downstairs to find me. He wanted to know what we were planning for supper. "Unplug the vacuum and call 911." The EMTs put me on a special two-piece stretcher and gave me a double dose of pain medication. Every little bump or shift was agonizing, especially going over railroad tracks on the way to the hospital emergency room. Getting on and off the x-ray table was too painful to describe. Finally, I went to surgery, received anesthesia and woke up with the pain gone. I went home the next morning and was surprised to find all the bruises on my arm and back where I had fallen on the vacuum. All went well for about three weeks.

But again, on a Thursday, during knitting class, it happened again. This time, all I did was raise up off my chair to reach for something and the hip popped out. Beside the pain, you could see that one leg was shorter than the other. My knitting students all moved into action. After calling 911, they got my pain meds and a jonnie from the bedroom. Together, they managed to remove my clothes so they wouldn't have to be cut off in the emergency room. At the hospital, I was anesthetized and again the hip was put back in place. The next morning, the surgeon informed me that I would have to have another hip replacement operation. "The ball has made a permanent groove in the socket and it's going to keep sliding out." I was scheduled for surgery on a Tuesday after a holiday weekend and didn't want to move a muscle all that time for fear my hip would dislocate yet again.

I was a little slower recovering the second time; again because of blood loss and being overly cautious. This second hip is not the same as the first. It tends to remind me if I'm doing something wrong or if there's a change in barometric pressure. The doctor says this new hip is good for thirty-five years. "That's more than I need," I told him. I think he realized I was a woman who needed

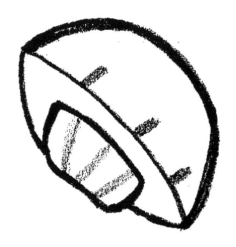

bigger balls. Here is a 3-D, actual size diagram of the first hip I received. I was very surprised to see how small a hip joint, that carries so much of the body's weight, really is.

If by any chance we must revert back to cave man times, count me out of the running for the next meal. I'll patiently wait by the fire with a recipe book deciding how cook the next catch.

CHAPTER 11

THE LAST WORD

My husband and I refer to us now in our golden years as being on the down slope. Even if you think and feel young, there are too many clues to remind you that you're not. First there's the notice that you're now eligible for Medicare. It becomes time to start collecting on your IRAs AND pay taxes on that money. Of course there are those aches and pains that pay you a visit at inopportune times. Then there is the matter of facial hair. You go to bed at night and the coast is clear. The next morning half-inch long hairs are sticking out of your chin. Even a balding man desiring a glorious mop wouldn't want those hairs. They are course, thick and stubborn. Last but not least, are the occasions when a salesclerk will ask if you are senior citizen. One time in Woolworth's I bought a jar of Pond's cold cream. At the checkout the clerk kindly asked, "And are we eligible for a senior discount today?" Now no one enjoys a bargain more than I do... but to be called a senior before one's time can be upsetting. I told my story to my friend, Ella. She said, "Anyone who buys Ponds cold cream *is* a senior citizen." Ella also claims that I always have to have the last word. It's true. I even plan to have the last word after I depart this world and move on to greener pastures. I believe I have many active and interesting years to look forward to, because I'm not done yet. However, it doesn't hurt to plan ahead. Here are my plans:

1. I have arranged to have my body donated to the University Medical School, where I earned my Masters and Doctorate degrees. I'll be available for studies by the medical students and they won't even have to use a pithing rod to get started.

2. Should my family decide to have a memorial service (or a celebration of my life); I should like it to be in a party-type atmosphere – perhaps at a country club. On that occasion, there should be large containers on wheels holding as much yarn as possible. At the end of the service, pallbearers should wheel the boxes out and announce, "Free yarn. Come and get it!"

3. Finally, I do not wish to have anyone saying dopey things about how wonderful I was! However, I do want someone special that I have in mind to read from the plaque that was presented to me by a graduating class at the university where I taught. This is what it said:

"Dr Giulia daMaglia, special guardian angel of freshmen, you have shepherded, prodded, believed in and advocated for all students of this University from your first days as a nursing professor to your last eight years as creator and director of the University Academic Advisement Program.

With characteristic vitality and vibrancy, you have dramatically and wondrously transformed the way the school provides for the needs of freshmen as well as for the needs of all entering students and those in academic transition. Out of your innovative ideas, your strong faculty influence, and your heartfelt concern that students not merely survive but flourish in their new collegiate environment, you developed the University's Academic Advising Center. Recruiting faculty advisors as caring as yourself, and keeping devoted and perceptive watch over your student charges, you have built a program remarkable for its success in turning potential school failures into triumphs. Adept at troubleshooting and gifted in making genuine connections of mutual trust, you have never hesitated to take the extra step to resolve a situation, a step that has often made the crucial difference in a student's college career.

We have prized you for many things, for your vision, as well as for your persistence and resourcefulness in bringing that vision to life, for your unfailing solicitude for our well-being, and for your love of life, of your job, and of us."

My favorite charity is the Shriners' Hospital for Crippled Children. Some of the proceeds from the sale of this book are to be donated to that wonderful charity. They have given help and hope to kids for over eighty years.

There! I have had the last word and I thank you for sharing some parts of my life and some of my thoughts with me!

APPENDIX A

Girl Scout Memorabilia

Intermediate Girl Scout Badge Sash

Girl Scout trip to Europe- charms from the countries and towns visited

Pin from Our Chalet- Switzerland   Pin from The Ark- London

First Class Award   Membership Pins (Brownies through Seniors)

Pin and Badge from Senior Roundup

APPENDIX B

Maglia's Methods for Moving Mountains

1. Divide and Conquer: Meet with influential people one at a time to open a door and be able to say, "Well, so and so thinks the plan has merit."

2. One Task to One Administrator: Engage only one boss to move the project. If you approach more than one, each will leave it to the other, and nothing will happen.

3. Use Facts and Drama: Start by explaining a predicament that tugs at the heart strings. Then present a printed copy of the facts.

4. Don't Ask Permission or Ask a Question that Allows a Yes or No Answer (Within Reason): If you ask, the answer will likely be 'no.'

5. Build up Credits: Do some work or favors for others. They will have a harder time rejecting your requests later.

6. Make a Move when Others are not Paying Attention or are Busy with Other Projects: Do not draw attention to yourself or look for praise.

7. Form Committees after the Fact: A committee organized to get a project off the ground wastes too much time defining everything. Committees formed when the project is underway will enjoy being part of a success story.

8. Protect the Boss's Image: Give him/her credit and praise that person for his/her helpfulness. You'll get your credit later!

9. Praise, Praise and Praise: Send thank you notes, memos, and letters of recommendation to or for anyone who helped in any way. That includes the secretaries and custodians.

10. Look the Part: Dress as if you're used to being successful.

11. Be Nosy: Ask people about themselves and remember what they say. Get to meet and know as many people in the institution, community or business as possible. This will lead to your being asked to be a part of projects where you can make an impact.

12. Don't Fight Battles You Cannot Win (Not even on principle): People will want to join you or your team if you are known to be a winner.

13. Put the Opposition Where You Know Where They Are: Put the person likely to give you the most grief on one of your committees so you will know what they are saying/thinking

14. Eliminate Fanfare: Don't draw attention to yourself. Stay in the background. Give other people the credit.

15. Seek Advice and Feedback: Ask for ideas. Listen. Be attentive. Accommodate suggested changes if it doesn't negatively affect the project.

16. Read the Literature and Network Entries: Pay attention to what works in other places.

17. Be Patient: Don't expect full support or full funding. Work your magic with what you get.

We the unwilling, led by the unqualified, have been doing the unbelievable for so long with so little, that we now attempt the impossible with nothing. (Anonymous)

APPENDIX C

A Brownie in a Box

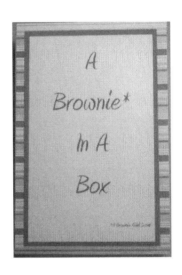

APPENDIX D

A Celebration of Cancer Survival

GIRLS JUST GOTTA HAVE FUN!!

Welcome in Song – Old Cape Cod

Fashion Show by Knitwits and Others

Narrator: Barbara

Models and Exhibitors:

Ellen	Pat
Noreen	Kathy
Barbara	Clay
Elaine	Cindy
Barbara	Judy
Kathy	Lorraine
Winifred	Priscilla

Response: You Must Have Been a Beautiful Baby

Breakfast Buffet

Entertainment

"Hey Soul Sister" - Choreographed and Danced by Barbara
"May you Always Have a Song" – Clay

Fancy Footwork by John
The Bunny Hop, The Chicken, YMCA, Twist and other requests
A Stroll through Judy's flower garden

A Time to Scratch

Other Stuff

Closing Message in Song "May You Always"

Old Cape Cod

If you're fond of sand dunes and salty air
  Quaint little villages here and there
You're sure to fall in love with Old Cape Cod.

If you like the taste of a lobster stew
  Served by a window with an ocean view
You're sure to fall in love with Old Cape Cod.

Winding roads that seem to beckon you
  Miles of green beneath the skies of blue
Church bells chiming on a Sunday morn
  Reminds you of the town where you were born
If you spend an evening you'd want to stay
  Watching the moonlight on Cape Cod Bay
You're sure to fall in love with Old Cape Cod.

You Must Have Been a Beautiful Baby

You must have been a beautiful baby
You must have been a wonderful child
When you were only startin' to go to kindergarten
I bet you drove the little boys wild

And when it came to winning blue ribbons
You must have showed the other kids how
I can see the judges' eyes as they handed you the prize
I bet you made the cutest bow

Oh you must have been a beautiful baby
'Cause baby look at you now

A White Sports Coat

A white sports coat and a pink carnation
I'm all dressed up for the dance
A white sports coat and a pink carnation
I'm all alone in romance

Once you told me long ago
To the prom with me you'd go
Now you've changed your mind it seems
Someone else will hold my dreams

A white sports coat and a pink carnation
I'm in a blue, blue mood
I'm all dressed up for the dance
I'm all alone in romance

Once you told me long ago
To the prom with me you'd go
Now you've changed your mind it seems
Someone else will hold my dreams

A white sports coat and a pink carnation
I'm in a blue, blue mood

May You Always Have a Song

May your life be filled with song
And may your friends all sing along
May your heart be true and strong
May you always have a song

May your life be filled with love
May the sun always shine above
Go in peace just like a dove
May you always have a song

May music be a part of the joy within your heart
May you feel it deep within your soul
May the gentle harmony of a tender melody make
your spirit whole

May your life be filled with song.
And may your friends all sing along.
May your heart be true and strong.
May you always have a song.
     (Pause)
May you always have a song.

May You Always

May you always walk in sunshine
Slumber warm when night winds blow
May you always live with laughter
For a smile becomes you so

May good fortune find your doorway
May the bluebird sing your song
May no trouble travel your way
May no worry stay too long

May your heartaches be forgotten
May no tears be spilled
May old acquaintance be remembered
And your cup of kindness filled

And may you always be a dreamer
May your wildest dreams come true
May you find someone to love
A much as I love you

May your heartaches be forgotten
May no tears be spilled
May old acquaintance be remembered
And your cup of kindness filled

And may you always be a dreamer
May your wildest dreams come true
May you find someone to love
As much as I love you

Made in the USA
Charleston, SC
14 June 2013